Lecture Notes in Computer Science 7165

Commenced Publication in 1973
Founding and Former Series Editors:
Gerhard Goos, Juris Hartmanis, and Jan van Leeuwen

T0213144

Alexis De Vos   Robert Wille (Eds.)

Reversible Computation

Third International Workshop, RC 2011
Gent, Belgium, July 4-5, 2011
Revised Papers

Springer

Volume Editors

Alexis De Vos
University of Gent
Sint Pietersnieuwstraat 41, 9000 Gent, Belgium
E-mail: alex@ELIS.UGent.be

Robert Wille
University of Bremen
Bibliothekstr. 1, 28215 Bremen, Germany
E-mail: rwille@informatik.uni-bremen.de

ISSN 0302-9743   e-ISSN 1611-3349
ISBN 978-3-642-29516-4   e-ISBN 978-3-642-29517-1
DOI 10.1007/978-3-642-29517-1
Springer Heidelberg Dordrecht London New York

Library of Congress Control Number: 2012935141

CR Subject Classification (1998): F.3, D.2, D.3, F.2, C.2, F.1

LNCS Sublibrary: SL 2 – Programming and Software Engineering

Typesetting: Camera-ready by author, data conversion by Scientific Publishing Services, Chennai, India

Printed on acid-free paper

Springer is part of Springer Science+Business Media (www.springer.com)

Preface

In recent years, reversible computation has established itself as a very promising research area and an emerging technology. This is motivated by a widely supported prediction that the conventional computer hardware technologies are going to reach their limits in the not-too-distant future.

In particular, the impact of power consumption of electronic devices on the intended behavior of such devices is becoming a serious problem. While the unwanted behavior of transistors can be reduced by higher levels of integration and new fabrication processes, a more fundamental problem exists: As proven by Landauer in 1961, each time a bit of information is deleted exactly $k \cdot T \cdot \log 2$ Joule of energy is dissipated, where k is the Boltzmann constant and T is the temperature. While this amount of energy does not seem presently significant, it forms potentially a barrier for future technologies. Transistors that perform millions of operations per second are fairly common these days, and more and more operations are performed on smaller and smaller transistors. Since these trends are most likely to continue, dissipation of $k \cdot T \cdot \log 2$ Joule of energy per bit of information lost will become crucial and may bring the progress of conventional computer technologies to a halt.

In contrast, reversible computations may reduce or even eliminate this power dissipation. This holds since n-input n-output functions, for some appropriate n, can be used to map each possible input vector to a unique output vector. Data are bijectively transformed in this way without losing any of the original information, thus avoiding energy dissipation. In fact, computations with zero power dissipation are only possible provided they are performed in a reversible manner. Thus, in order to overcome the limitations caused by Landauer's barrier, computation has to be reversible.

Moreover, quantum computation has become a major application area for reversible logic. It uses qubits instead of the conventional bits. Qubits allow one to represent not only 0 and 1 but also a superposition of both. As a result, qubits can represent multiple states at the same time theoretically enabling enormous speed-ups in computation. It has been shown that, for example, using a quantum circuit it is possible to solve the factorization problem in polynomial time while for conventional circuits only exponential methods exist. Admittedly, although the research in the domain of quantum circuits is still in its infancy, the first simple quantum circuits are being physically implemented. Reversible computation is therefore essential because every quantum operation is inherently reversible. Thus, progress in the domain of reversible logic can be directly applied to quantum logic.

Further applications of reversible computation paradigms can be found in coding/decoding, program debugging, testing, database recovery, discrete event simulation, reversible algorithms, reversible specification formalisms, reversible programming languages, process algebras and semantics of concurrency, or the modeling of biochemical systems.

The Workshop on Reversible Computation provides a platform to present and to discuss new trends and recent developments in this promising area. Previous events took place in March 2009 in York, UK (with proceedings published as ENTCS Volume 253, Issue 6) and in July 2010 in Bremen, Germany (with proceedings published in the *Journal of Multiple-Valued Logic and Soft Computing* Volume 18, Issue 1).

The volume at hand covers revised and extended versions of the best papers presented at the third edition of the Workshop on Reversible Computation which took place in Gent, Belgium, during July 4–5, 2011. From a total of 25 original submissions, the Program Committee selected 10 submissions for publication in this issue (leading to an acceptance rate of 40%). For this purpose, an intensive double-blind review process was conducted.

The first paper considers a theoretical aspect of reversible computation. The author H.B. Axelsen studies the time complexity of tape reduction in reversible Turing machines. While it was already known that the reduction from k tapes to 1 tape in general leads to a quadratic increase in time, for k to 2 tapes a reduction to a logarithmic factor is possible.

Ways toward a functional language for reversible computations are described in the second paper. T. Yokoyama, H.B. Axelsen, and R. Glück identify the basic concepts such a language has to satisfy and discuss the advantages using several example programs.

Logic design is considered in the following three papers. M.K. Thomsen, H.B. Axelsen, and R. Glück describe the design of a purely reversible processor architecture and its instruction set. Therefore, a simple, yet expressive, locally invertible instruction set, and fully reversible control logic and address calculation, is applied. Optimization techniques for reversible circuits based on templates are introduced by M.M. Rahman, G.W. Dueck, and A. Banerjee, who make use of a newly developed splitting rule. Finally, C. Moraga presents an extension of the commonly used Toffoli gates enabling one to efficiently realize operations in GF(2) and lattice operations of a Boolean algebra.

The sixth paper presents a software toolkit called RevKit that assists users in the design of reversible circuits. RevKit is developed by M. Soeken, S. Frehse, R. Wille, and R. Drechsler. It provides various functionalities ranging from synthesis and optimization to verification of reversible circuits. Furthermore, RevKit is open source so that other researchers can use and extend its functionalities.

The application of reversible computation to the domain of quantum circuits is covered in the seventh and eighth paper. Z. Sasanian and D.M. Miller propose a mapping of reversible gate into quantum gates using the NCVW library instead of the previously applied NCV library. Afterwards, quantum circuit synthesis considering linear nearest neighbor architectures is considered by A. Matsuo and S. Yamashita.

Finally, physical realizations of reversible circuits in CMOS technologies is the subject of the last two papers. First, S. Burignat, M. Olczak, M. Klimczak, and

A. De Vos discuss key questions rising from existing reversible dual-line pass-transistor technology. Afterwards, a technical solution that allows interfacing reversible pass-transistor logic with conventional CMOS logic is presented by S. Burignat, M.K. Thomsen, M. Klimczak, M. Olczak, and A. De Vos.

We would like to thank all the authors for their valuable contributions to this special issue devoted to RC 2011. Furthermore, many thanks are due to the members of the Program Committee and all external reviewers for their excellent work in evaluating the submissions as well as for providing detailed feedback and further suggestions to the authors. Finally, we wish to thank Alfred Hofmann of Springer for agreeing to publish these proceedings in the book series Springer *Lecture Notes in Computer Science*. Support from the University of Ghent and the University of Bremen is also gratefully acknowledged.

November 2011

Alexis De Vos
Robert Wille

Table of Contents

Time Complexity of Tape Reduction
for Reversible Turing Machines

Holger Bock Axelsen

DIKU, Department of Computer Science, University of Copenhagen
funkstar@diku.dk

Abstract. Studies of reversible Turing machines (RTMs) often differ in their use of *static resources* such as the number of tapes, symbols and internal states. However, the interplay between such resources and computational complexity is not well-established for RTMs. In particular, many foundational results in reversible computing theory are about multitape machines with two or more tapes, but it is non-obvious what these results imply for reversible complexity theory.

Here, we study how the time complexity of multitape RTMs behaves under reductions to one and two tapes. For deterministic Turing machines, it is known that the reduction from k tapes to 1 tape in general leads to a quadratic increase in time. For k to 2 tapes, a celebrated result shows that the time overhead can be reduced to a logarithmic factor. We show that identical results hold for multitape RTMs.

This establishes that the structure of reversible time complexity classes mirrors that of irreversible complexity theory, with a similar hierarchy.

1   Introduction

Turing machines are very robust with respect to variations in static resources: adding extra symbols, tracks, tapes, or the like does not add any functions or languages to the computable set. While there is no impact on computability, the effect on *computational complexity* can be profound. In a series of classic papers, Hartmanis, Hennie, and Stearns [4, 5, 6] established the effect on time complexity of tape reduction for deterministic Turing machines (DTMs). Tape reduction strictly diminishes the class of problems that we can solve within a given (asymptotic) time bound, which shows the existence of a time hierarchy for DTMs. On the other hand, there are also many complexity classes (such as P) which are themselves robust under tape reduction.

It is known that the reversible Turing machines (RTMs) are equally robust computability-wise wrt the number of symbols, tracks and tapes [2, 11]. However, the analogous complexity results are *not* well-established for RTMs. This limits the generality of statements regarding *reversible complexity*. Complexity classes are (usually) defined for 1-tape machines, but many foundational results in reversible computing theory use *multitape* machines. As a familiar example, the Landauer embedding [8], which is integral to Bennett's method [3], yields a

A. De Vos and R. Wille (Eds.): RC 2011, LNCS 7165, pp. 1–13, 2012.

2-tape RTM that recognizes the same language as a given 1-tape TM. Despite this, it is not at all obvious what the 2-tape machine can tell us about the reversible complexities of this language, since this requires a 1-tape machine. Thus, knowing the complexity-wise effects of varying static resources is both useful and necessary for developing complexity theory for reversible Turing machines.[1]

Here, we examine the effect on *time complexity* of *tape reduction* for RTMs (Section 2). By adapting well-known irreversible tape reductions to work reversibly, we show that tape reductions can be as time-efficient for RTMs as they are for DTMs. We give two main results: first, k-to-1 tape reduction (Section 3) can be done at quadratic cost in running time, in that a $t(n)$ time computation with k tapes can be performed in $\mathcal{O}(t(n)^2)$ time with 1 tape. Like with DTMs we show that this is optimal: some computations are $\Omega(n^2)$ time for 1-tape RTMs, but $\mathcal{O}(n)$ time for 2-tape RTMs, so the quadratic increase in simulation time cannot be improved in general. Second, k-to-2 tape reduction (Section 4) can be done with only a log factor overhead, in that a $t(n)$ time computation with a k-tape machine can be performed in $\mathcal{O}(t(n) \log t(n))$ steps with 2 tapes.

2   Reversible Turing Machines

In this paper we consider multitape reversible Turing machines (RTMs). We assume familiarity with RTMs, and shall only briefly describe them here. We refer the reader to [2, 3, 11] for more complete expositions.

A Turing machine is *reversible* iff it is forward and backward deterministic. This intuitively means that at most one rule from the machine's transition function can be applied to any given configuration (forward determinism), and at most one rule leads to any given configuration (backward determinism).

We use a triple format for the rules of the k-tape RTMs in this paper, with two distinct kinds of rule. A *symbol rule* $(q, (s, t), p)$ says that in state q, if the tape heads read symbols $s \in \Sigma^k$ (where Σ is a finite alphabet), write symbols $t \in \Sigma^k$ and change into state p. A *move rule* (q, d, p) says that in state q, move the k tape heads in the directions given by $d \in \{\leftarrow, \downarrow, \rightarrow\}^k$ and change into state p. A machine is *backward deterministic* iff for any distinct pair of rules (q_1, a_1, p_1) and (q_2, a_2, p_2), if $p_1 = p_2$ then $a_1 = (s_1, t_1)$, $a_2 = (s_2, t_2)$, and $t_1 \neq t_2$.

We are mostly concerned with RTMs for decision problems, and in particular their time complexity. We define the *reversible time complexity class* $\mathsf{RevTIME}_k(t(n))$ to be the set of all languages that are decidable[2] by an $\mathcal{O}(t(n))$ time RTM with k work tapes, where n is the length of the input given on one of the work tapes. This is completely analogous to the definition of $\mathsf{DTIME}_k(t(n))$ for deterministic (but not necessarily reversible) TMs. Note that we trivially have $\mathsf{RevTIME}_k(t(n)) \subseteq \mathsf{DTIME}_k(t(n))$ for any number of tapes k and time bound $t(\cdot)$. For single-tape machines ($k = 1$) we shall omit the subscript.

---

[1] This is still the case if we instead define time complexity by multitape machines.

[2] *Decider* machines halt in an accepting state '*yes*' for all strings in some language; and halt in a reject state '*no*' for all others. *Recognizer* machines (sometimes also called *acceptors* or *semi-deciders*) may diverge on strings not in the language.

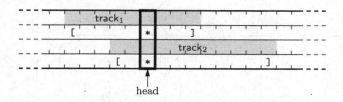

Fig. 1. Track layout for 1-tape simulation of 2-tape Turing machines. Two tracks (track$_1$ and track$_2$) simulate the 2 tapes. On auxiliary tracks, delimiters [and] give the extent of the non-blank tape contents (grey squares), and markers * show the simulated tape head positions. After realigning the tracks, these markers always match up.

3 One-Tape Simulation of Multitape RTMs

Hartmanis and Stearns [4] showed that a k-tape Turing machine T_k with running time $t(n)$ can be simulated by a 1-tape TM T_1 with running time $\mathcal{O}(t(n)^2)$. The idea of the simulation is to turn the k tapes into $\mathcal{O}(k)$ *tracks*, with delimiters for the 'ends' of the tapes and markers for the simulated tape heads, as seen in Figure 1. If a multitape rule has the tape heads move differently, *e.g.* $(q, \left[\overset{\rightarrow}{\underset{\leftarrow}{}} \right], p)$, the simulated rule realigns the tracks such that the markers (*) line up again:

$$q \longrightarrow \boxed{\text{move marks}} \longrightarrow \boxed{\text{shift track}_1 \text{ left}} \rightarrow \boxed{\text{shift track}_2 \text{ right}} \longrightarrow p$$

The slowdown comes from the fact that shifting the tracks one cell to the left or right takes time linear in their size, and this is done $\mathcal{O}(t(n))$ times. Recently, we applied this idea to RTMs [2]. Importantly, the overhead induced by reversibility does not influence the asymptotic complexities, in that we can still shift the tracks in linear time.

Proposition 1. *A k-tape reversible Turing machine with running time $t(n)$ can be simulated by a 1-tape reversible Turing with running time $\mathcal{O}(t(n)^2)$.*

This establishes an upper bound for general simulation of multitape RTMs.

For DTMs Hennie [5] provided a lower bound matching the upper bound for 1-tape simulation of just 2 tapes. Hennie considers the language

$$L = \{w2^n w \in \{0, 1, 2\}^* \mid w \in \{0, 1\}^n, n > 0\},$$

consisting of strings that repeat a binary word w twice, separated by a block of 2's as long as w itself. The first part of the proof shows a 1-tape TM that decides L in $\mathcal{O}(n^2)$ time, where n is the length of the input. The second part proves that the language L requires at least quadratic time for 1-tape TMs[3] on the 'yes' instances (so the $\mathcal{O}(n^2)$ upper bound is tight). The third part of

---

[3] In Hennie's and our TM model the input is given on the single work tape. If the input is instead given on a separate read-only (left-to-right) input tape, then the lower bound still holds but is considerably harder to obtain [10].

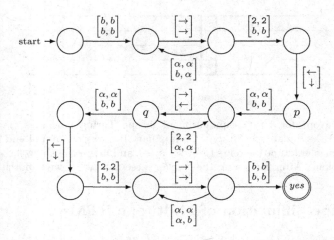

Fig. 2. State transition diagram for a 2-tape RTM that recognizes the language L. Edges with the symbolic variable α are used to signify the two rules for $\alpha \in \{0, 1\}$, and b is the blank symbol.

the proof shows that the language L is decidable by a 2-tape TM in linear time (which is also asymptotically optimal). This shows that the simulation by Hartmanis and Stearns in optimal in general.

This is also the case for RTMs, but in order to prove it we have to replicate each part of Hennie's proof for RTMs. First, we remark that the lower bounds (linear time for 2-tape machines, quadratic time for 1-tape machines) trivially apply to RTMs as well, because the RTMs are a proper subset of the DTMs. However, note that this is not in itself sufficient to show the desired result, because we have not yet established that these lower bounds are *tight* for RTMs. Second, if we can find a 2-tape RTM that decides L in linear time, then we get the quadratic time 1-tape machine for free, simply by applying the 1-tape simulation of 2-tape RTMs. In fact, because the bounds apply specifically to the accepted inputs, a recognizer, rather than a decider, is sufficient. Thus, the entire proof reduces to finding such a machine.

Proposition 2. *There exists a 2-tape RTM that recognizes L in time $\mathcal{O}(n)$.*

Proof. Let the string $l \in \{0, 1, 2\}^*$ be given on the first tape in standard configuration form, *i.e.*, with the tape head to the immediate left of l, and the rest of the tape(s) blank. To decide whether l is in L we follow Hennie's idea: copy the binary word w to the second tape; rewind the second tape while passing over the 2's on the first tape; compare the binary word on the first tape with the copy on the second. Of course, the machine now has to do this reversibly, which complicates matters somewhat, but the basic idea holds. Figure 2 shows an RTM that recognizes L in linear time.   □

We can therefore conclude that 1-tape RTM simulation of multitape RTMs has exactly the same time complexity bounds as 1-tape DTM simulation of

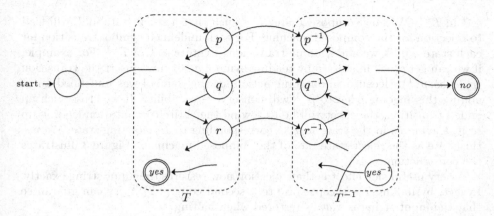

Fig. 3. Composition of T and T^{-1} to eliminate stuck states. The arcs from T to T^{-1} denote the extra symbol rules we add to avoid getting stuck. Note that the inverse image of T's accept state is unreachable.

multitape DTMs. This opens the door for a host of useful and immediate results for reversible complexity theory. For instance, since we have multi-tape universal RTMs that simulate 1-tape machines with constant factor overheads [2,1], standard techniques can be used to show that the reversible Turing machines have a time hierarchy, in a manner completely analogous to DTMs [4]. Furthermore, the Landauer embedding (generalized to k-tape machines) can now be used to show that $\bigcup_k \mathsf{DTIME}_k(t(n)) \subseteq \mathsf{RevTIME}(t(n)^2)$. As a final example, just as P is robust under tape reduction, so is its reversible analogue RevP (defined in the obvious manner).

3.1 Eliminating Stuck States from RTMs

The L-recognizer above gets stuck on all strings that are not in L, *e.g.* at states p and q, rather than rejecting or diverging (running forever). This means that there are two kinds of non-halting behavior: infinite loops and stuck states. To avoid ambiguity it is very often required that machines will *never* get stuck.

It is only possible to get stuck in a state q in some TM T if q does not have outgoing symbol rules for all symbols in the tape alphabet. For irreversible DTMs we can avoid stuck states by simply adding dummy transitions to the reject state for every such undefined transition. For reversible machines this will not work: there is only one reject state, and backward determinism limits the number of transitions into any state to the size of the alphabet. There may be many more stuck states than we can differentiate in this way. A naïve solution could be to expand the (internal) alphabet to include enough symbols to differentiate all the reject transitions we need to add, but this is a somewhat inelegant and wasteful use of resources.

A key feature of RTMs is that they are very easily inverted, cf. [3,2]. Let T^{-1} be the inverse of T, but with the convention that all states q are renamed to

q^{-1} in T^{-1}. We now compose T and T^{-1} such that a stuck state in T will lead to rejection for the composed machine. For each undefined symbol transition for each state q in T we add dummy transitions to state q^{-1} in T^{-1}. For example, if we can get stuck in state p by reading symbol a, then we insert the transition $(p, (a, a), p^{-1})$. Because an outgoing action for this symbol was undefined for p, adding this ingoing edge to p^{-1} will conserve reversibility. If we cross such an added transition, the effect will be to rewind the entire computation leading up to it, leaving us in the state in T^{-1} corresponding to T's starting state. We use this state as the reject state '*no*' of the composed machine.[4] Figure 3 illustrates the construction.

A very useful side effect is that rejection now restores the input string exactly. In fact, by linking T's accept state to a second copy of T^{-1}, we can guarantee that the input string is *always* restored when halting.

In this way it can be ensured that RTMs never get stuck, so we can assume wlog that the only non-halting behavior is running forever. An interesting consequence is that we can then also assume that space-bounded RTMs always halt. Also note that the construction preserves the complexities of the original machine. As a final remark, the author used essentially this construction to implement string comparison in a universal RTM [1].

4   Two-Tape Simulation of Multitape RTMs

Hennie and Stearns [6] showed the beautiful result that a k-tape machine T_k with running time $t(n)$ can be simulated by a 2-tape Turing machine T_2 with only a logarithmic factor slowdown, so that T_2 has running time $\mathcal{O}(t(n) \log t(n))$. Does a similar result hold for the RTMs?

A logarithmic factor is indeed achievable for multitape RTM simulation with only a fixed number of simulation tapes. We can instrument a 2-tape Hennie-Stearns simulation of a k-tape RTM with a Landauer embedding: this yields a 3-tape RTM simulation of the k-tape RTM with only logarithmic factor slowdown.[5]

Thus, only the time complexity of 2-tape reversible simulation of multitape RTMs remains undecided. The rest of this paper is devoted to resolving this problem, by adapting the Hennie-Stearns simulation for reversibility.

4.1   The Hennie-Stearns Simulation

We outline the ideas of the Hennie-Stearns simulation below. For exact details and proofs we refer to the original paper [6], which is still eminently readable.

Layout. The tapes of T_k are each simulated with two tracks placed on one of T_2's tapes (the other tape is for scratch space). A simulated tape is 'horizontally' divided into two *levels* (the two tracks), and 'vertically' into *areas* numbered

---

[4] If T already has a reject state a dummy move transition targeting its image state in T^{-1} can be added.

[5] It is possible to remove the added trace by Bennett's method for injective functions.

$1, 2, 3, 4, \ldots$ of $1, 2, 4, 8, \ldots$ cells each, on both sides of a designated *home column* H (where the simulated heads of T_k point to). Thus, the ith area on either side has space for 2^i symbols in both levels combined.

The contents of a simulated tape consists of each non-empty area in sequence, first lower levels then upper levels (ignoring empty area levels) reading from the left towards the home column. Symmetrically, from the home column towards the right we read upper levels first, followed by lower levels, for each area. Figure 4(a) shows how to read a simulated tape under this layout.

There are a number of invariants to respect for each simulated tape.

- Each level of each storage area is either completely full or empty.
- The lower level of the home column (the *home square*) is always full, and the upper level always empty.
- If the upper level of an area is full, then so is the lower level *and* the 'mirror' area on the other side of the home column must be empty.
- If the lower level of an area is empty, then so is the upper level *and* the 'mirror' area on the other side of the home column must be completely full.
- At the beginning of the simulation, all lower levels are full, and all upper levels are empty.[6]

This guarantees that the ith right (left) storage area always has space to accommodate the entire non-empty content of the lower-numbered areas to the right (left) of the home square. (Note that a lower level can be full and the upper level empty. Also note that we can have filled lower levels in both right and left area i without breaking the invariants.)

Cleanup. To simulate a move rule, the central idea is to shift only *parts* of the simulated tapes around by using the upper levels as extra storage. For the rest of the paper, assume that we want to simulate rule $(q, [\leftarrow, \cdots], p)$, *i.e.*, that a tape head moves left. We must then shift the simulated tape to the right, which is done as follows.

1. From the home column, find the first non-empty left area, number i.
2a. If the upper level of this area is full, move the upper level's content into the empty lower levels of the $i - 1$ first left areas, with the rightmost symbol going into the home square.
2b. Else, move the lower level of area i in the same way.
3. Collect the original home square symbol and the contents in both levels of the first $i - 1$ *right* areas (these are all full), and place the first half of the content in the lower levels of the first $i - 1$ right areas.
4a. If the lower level of the ith right area is empty, place the second half there.
4b. Else, place the remaining symbols in the (empty) upper level of this area.
5. Return to the home column, and continue with the next simulated tape.

This procedure is called a *cleanup of order i*, and can be executed by the 2-tape DTM in time $\mathcal{O}(2^i)$, *i.e.*, *linearly* in the number of moved symbols. This is key

---

[6] This means that blank squares from T_k are *not* the same as empty squares in T_2.

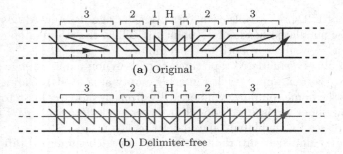

(a) Original

(b) Delimiter-free

Fig. 4. Layout of a tape simulated with two tracks. The storage areas are numbered around the home column H. (a) shows how to read off the contents of the tape in the original layout by Hennie and Stearns, and (b) shows our modified layout. In both layouts empty squares should be ignored in the reading.

to proving the time bound: the procedure guarantees that high-order cleanups will be very rare compared to low-order cleanups, and this leads to a logarithmic (rather than linear) time factor overhead for the simulation.

4.2   Reversible Cleanup Implementation

Now, can we implement the cleanup procedure reversibly?

The key idea of the implementation is to use the scratch tape for several purposes. To find the ith left area, we move the simulation tape head to the left until we encounter a non-empty cell: this cell is the right end of area i. At the same time, we also move the scratch tape head to mark out 2^{i-1} cells. This is exactly the length of area i, and also exactly as many symbols as we need to move into the lower order areas. We can also recognize the left end of area i by moving the scratch head back across the markings, while moving the simulation tape head to the left. Thus, the marked scratch space can be used to move exactly the number of symbols we need, in each step of the procedure.

Moving n contiguous symbols n places can easily be done in linear time by RTMs with 2 tapes. It is not difficult to see how to adapt this to the particular kinds of moves we need, and we assume these for the rest of the implementation.

We have identified three main sources of irreversibility in the cleanup procedure, all of which can be dealt with while preserving the time complexity.

Block delimiters. In step 3, we need delimiters to mark the extent of *each* area we visit, in order to move the content from the simulation tape onto the scratch tape in the correct order. In the original implementation delimiters are placed at run-time, but we cannot do this reversibly without knowing by other means whether a delimiter should be placed or not.

Solution. Delimiters can be avoided by changing the tape layout slightly. We adopt a uniform *down/up* reading for each *cell*, rather than for each *area level* (symmetrically, *up/down* to the right of the home column), as shown in Figure 4(b). It is now straightforward to move the home square and right areas onto the scratch tape in the correct order *without* using delimiters between areas.

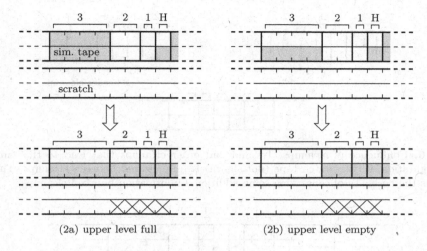

(2a) upper level full   (2b) upper level empty

Fig. 5. Resolving intermediate control flow confluence in step 2 of a 3rd order cleanup. Grey squares are filled, white squares are empty. The two branches are orthogonal by whether area 3 (identified by markings on the scratch tape) is empty or not.

Intermediate control confluence. There is control flow confluence in step 2, when moving the upper level (2a) or lower level (2b) of the ith left area. The control flow of these two branches must be merged reversibly before step 3, which requires finding an orthogonal property to distinguish them by. The same problem occurs at the end of step 4.

Solution. We can orthogonalize the two branches by examining the rightmost cell of area i: its lower level is filled if we came from (2a), and empty if we came from (2b). This requires that we can tell where area i is, which means remembering the value i somehow. This is done by keeping the marks we placed on the scratch tape while finding area i, after steps (2a) and (2b), see Figure 5.

Cleanup confluence. The control flow confluence applies to cleanups in general: different order cleanups can lead to identical simulated tapes, as shown in Figure 6, and we can only tell these apart by remembering the order i of the cleanup. This is an inherent trait of the Hennie-Stearns simulation: the restoration of the standard reading in all the lower order blocks after a high order cleanup is essential for keeping the time complexity low.

Solution. The marked space on the scratch tape (a unary representation of 2^{i-1}) can be conserved, by always marking space towards the *right*, for simulating *both* left and right shifts. This ensures that we never move more than one cell to the left of the position of the scratch head at the start of a cleanup. After a cleanup has been performed, we then move the scratch head across the (conserved) markings and past the following blank square, to prepare for the next cleanup. Thus, the scratch tape is still used to perform linear time moves, but also stores a history of the previous markings, which defines the *orders* of the cleanups performed, see Figure 7. This is sufficient for reversibility.

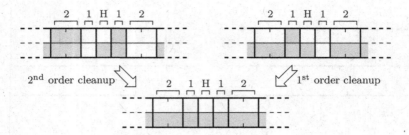

Fig. 6. Confluence of cleanups: 1st and 2nd order cleanups that lead to the same configuration, if the scratch tape (not shown) is fully cleared between cleanups. This shows the necessity of conserving some additional information between cleanups.

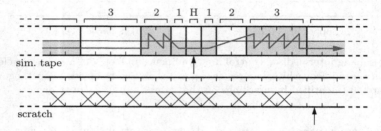

Fig. 7. The configuration of the 2-tape simulation after 4 left cleanups (of orders 1, 2, 1 and 3) and then 2 right cleanups (orders 1 and 2). When simulating multiple tapes, the orders of cleanups from the individual tapes will be interleaved on the scratch tape.

It is only the markings on the scratch tape that we cannot remove—the rest of the procedure works reversibly. While we do use a partial trace, importantly, it does *not* require an extra tape, like the Landauer embedding does. If desired (*e.g.* for function problems) this *order trace* can be removed by standard reversible computing methods, see Appendix A.

4.3   Reversible Time Complexity

None of the above solutions affect the time complexity of an ith order cleanup.

The novel delimiter-free layout requires that we implement the movement of symbols somewhat differently from the original version: in step (2a) we have to 'smooth out' left area i which is completely filled, and in step (4b) we have to 'fold up' right area i to fill it completely. By using a two-track scratch tape, this can be done with a constant number of passes, which conserves complexity. How this works is shown in Figure 8. Of course, this layout can also be used to obviate block delimiters in the irreversible simulation.

Conserving the marked space on the scratch tape during a cleanup adds no time overhead. Finally, passing over these marks to prepare the scratch tape for the next cleanup is also only linear in the number of marked cells.

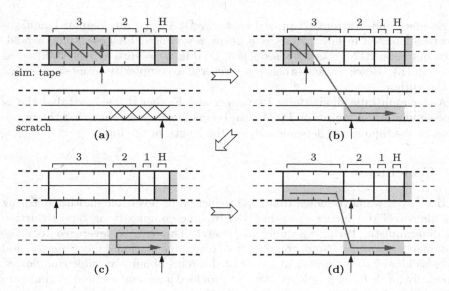

Fig. 8. Smoothing a tape reading in step (2a) of a 3rd order cleanup. To start with (a), the simulation tape has both levels of area 3 full, so we (b) move the first half into the lower level of the marked space on the scratch tape. We know when we have come halfway, because we run out of marks on the scratch tape. Then we (c) move the second half into the upper level on the scratch tape, and (d) move the upper level of the scratch level back into the lower level of area 3 of the simulation tape. This requires three passes of the area, regardless of its length.

We conclude that performing an ith order *reversible* cleanup takes time $\mathcal{O}(2^i)$. This matches the time complexity of the irreversible cleanup. Thus, the same argument used by Hennie and Stearns for the time complexity of their simulation applies to our reversible simulation of multitape RTMs.

Proposition 3. *A k-tape reversible Turing machine with running time $t(n)$ can be simulated by a 2-tape reversible Turing machine in $\mathcal{O}(t(n) \log t(n))$ time.*

This can, again, be used to elicit many further reversible complexity results. For instance, we now know that adding extra tapes to RTMs at most shaves off a logarithmic factor on any time bounds for multitape machines. Furthermore, the reversible Turing machines have an even tighter time hierarchy than before. Also, by Landauer embedding k-tape DTMs and applying the above 2-tape reversible simulation we have that $\bigcup_k \mathsf{DTIME}_k(t(n)) \subseteq \mathsf{RevTIME}_2(t(n) \log t(n))$.

5   Related Work

Most other work on reversible complexity has focused on space, time and energy trade-offs for reversible simulations of irreversible computations. Well-known results includes reversible simulation using pebble games, *e.g.* [14], and the (surprising) result that $\mathsf{RevSPACE}(s(n)) = \mathsf{DSPACE}(s(n))$ [9].

Kondacs and Watrous [7] proved that any DFA (*i.e.*, any regular language) can be simulated in linear time by a 2-way reversible DFA (essentially a read-only, one-tape RTM). As a consequence, $\mathsf{DTIME}(n) = \mathsf{REG} = \mathsf{RevTIME}(n)$, as noted in [13]. However, few other 'pure' reversible complexity results are known to the author.

As for multitape simulations, Pippenger and Fischer [12] showed that the 2-tape simulation of multitape DTMs can be made *oblivious*, such that the movement of the tape heads depends only on the length of the input.

6   Conclusion

In this paper we have shown that tape reduction of reversible multitape Turing machines (RTMs) incurs the same cost in time complexity as tape reduction for deterministic Turing machines in general. This can be leveraged to make statements about the (time) complexity of reversible machines more precise, and gives us almost direct access to a host of theorems about reversible complexity, especially for decision problems. We also provided a general method to eliminate stuck states from RTMs at no cost in complexity.

Adapting the Hennie-Stearns 2-tape simulation for reversibility required the use of a partial trace. No extra tape was needed for this; it can easily be removed from the final configuration, and it does not affect the time complexity of the simulation. However, it adds a time-dependent space overhead to the simulation that the 1-tape simulation does not. It is almost certainly possible to compress the trace at runtime, but avoiding a trace altogether appears doubtful.

We close with an open question. It is known that linear reversible and deterministic time are equal. Is reversible time equal to deterministic time *in general* for single-tape Turing machines, *i.e.*, is $\mathsf{RevTIME}(t(n)) = \mathsf{DTIME}(t(n))$?

Acknowledgements. The author would like to thank Michael Kirkedal Thomsen, Thomas Pécseli, and Robert Glück for comments on a draft of this paper.

References

1. Axelsen, H.B., Glück, R.: A Simple and Efficient Universal Reversible Turing Machine. In: Dediu, A.-H., Inenaga, S., Martín-Vide, C. (eds.) LATA 2011. LNCS, vol. 6638, pp. 117–128. Springer, Heidelberg (2011)
2. Axelsen, H.B., Glück, R.: What Do Reversible Programs Compute? In: Hofmann, M. (ed.) FOSSACS 2011. LNCS, vol. 6604, pp. 42–56. Springer, Heidelberg (2011)
3. Bennett, C.H.: Logical reversibility of computation. IBM J. Res. Dev. 17, 525–532 (1973)
4. Hartmanis, J., Stearns, R.E.: On the computational complexity of algorithms. Trans. Amer. Math. Soc. 117, 285–306 (1965)
5. Hennie, F.: One-tape, off-line Turing machine computations. Inform. Control 8, 553–578 (1965)
6. Hennie, F., Stearns, R.E.: Two-tape simulation of multitape Turing machines. J. ACM 13(4), 533–546 (1966)

7. Kondacs, A., Watrous, J.: On the power of quantum finite state automata. In: Proc. Foundations of Computer Science, pp. 66–75. IEEE (1997)
8. Landauer, R.: Irreversibility and heat generation in the computing process. IBM J. Res. Dev. 5(3), 183–191 (1961)
9. Lange, K.J., McKenzie, P., Tapp, A.: Reversible space equals deterministic space. J. Comput. Syst. Sci. 60(2), 354–367 (2000)
10. Maass, W.: Combinatorial lower bound arguments for deterministic and nondeterministic Turing machines. Trans. Amer. Math. Soc. 292(2), 675–693 (1985)
11. Morita, K., Shirasaki, A., Gono, Y.: A 1-tape 2-symbol reversible Turing machine. Trans. IEICE E 72(3), 223–228 (1989)
12. Pippenger, N., Fischer, M.J.: Relations among complexity measures. J. ACM 26(2), 361–381 (1979)
13. Tadaki, K., Yamakami, T., Lin, J.C.H.: Theory of one-tape linear-time Turing machines. Theor. Comput. Sci. 411(1), 22–43 (2010)
14. Vitányi, P.: Time, space, and energy in reversible computing. In: Proc. Computing Frontiers, pp. 435–444. ACM (2005)
15. Yokoyama, T., Axelsen, H.B., Glück, R.: Optimizing reversible simulation of injective functions. J. Mult.-Val. Log. S. 18(1), 5–24 (2012)

A Removing the Trace

The order trace is an unwanted side effect of the simulation. There is the additional problem that we are not guaranteed that the simulated tapes have a 'smooth' contiguous structure at the end of the simulation, with the output string in only the lower levels of the areas. To solve this problem we can use a modified version of clean simulation of injective functions [15], as follows.

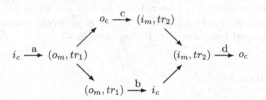

Run the simulation forwards (a) and extract a contiguous output copy o_c (placed on extra tracks) from the 'messy' output o_m. Run the simulation backwards (b), restoring the input in contiguous form, i_c, and removing the (partial) trace tr_1. Now run the simulation of the *inverse* machine on the contiguous output (c). The contiguous input i_c from (b) can be merged into the resulting 'messy' input i_m from (c). Finally, run the simulation of the inverse machine backwards (d), which removes the (partial) trace tr_2 resulting in only the contiguous output o_c.

Towards a Reversible Functional Language

Tetsuo Yokoyama[1], Holger Bock Axelsen[2], and Robert Glück[2]

[1] Department of Software Engineering, Nanzan University
tyokoyama@acm.org
[2] DIKU, Department of Computer Science, University of Copenhagen
funkstar@diku.dk, glueck@acm.org

Abstract. We identify concepts of reversibility for a functional language by means of a set of semantic rules with specific properties. These properties include injectivity along with local backward determinism, an important operational property for an efficient reversible language. We define a concise reversible first-order functional language in which access to the backward semantics is provided to the programmer by inverse function calls. Reversibility guarantees that in this language a backward run (inverse interpretation) is as fast as the corresponding forward run itself. By adopting a *symmetric first-match* policy for case expressions, we can write overlapping patterns in case branches, as is customary in ordinary functional languages, and also in leaf expressions, unlike existing inverse interpreter methods, which enables concise programs. In patterns, the use of a duplication/equality operator also simplifies inverse computation and program inversion. We discuss the advantages of a reversible functional language using example programs, including run-length encoding. Program inversion is seen to be as lightweight as for imperative reversible languages and realized by recursive descent. Finally, we show that the proposed language is *r-Turing complete*.

1 Introduction

Functional languages provide a natural and general mechanism for manipulating structured data, associated with powerful pattern-matching features and abstract data types. They also enable higher-level abstractions than imperative languages and thus more concise programs with the same functionality. For these reasons it is interesting to apply such a well-established language paradigm to reversibility. We aim to develop a reversible functional language for studying the foundations of reversible programming.

From the viewpoint of reversibility, functional programming enforces us to take a more rigorous and restricted approach than in existing work. For example, the imperative reversible language Janus [12,18] allows irreversible arithmetic and logical operators in expressions, and these do not have bidirectionality between input and output. In pure functional languages, it is more natural to describe natural numbers using only declarative fundamental features, *e.g.* based on the Peano axioms. This approach forces us to use only purely reversible

A. De Vos and R. Wille (Eds.): RC 2011, LNCS 7165, pp. 14–29, 2012.

language constructions, which is suitable for developing both basic theory and general concepts for reversible computing.

The contribution of this paper is to identify a concept of reversibility in a functional language setting and specify a purely-reversible and purely-functional language. Reversible computation of injective functions can be regarded as a case of inverse interpretation [1]. Because general solutions to inverse interpretation, *e.g.* McCarthy's generate-and-test [13], are often inefficient in practice, our interest lies in finding a solution by constructing a programming language which has efficient inverse computation built in by design.

Injectivity of the function implemented by a program is not sufficient for *efficient* inverse interpretation; backward deterministic control flow is also required. Consider the function *inc*, which takes a natural number n as argument and returns $n+1$ in the form of Peano numbers, where Z denotes zero and $S(n)$ denotes the successor of n. A straightforward implementation is:

$$inc\ n \triangleq \textbf{case } n \textbf{ of}$$
$$Z \quad \rightarrow \underline{S(Z)} \qquad\qquad (1)$$
$$S(n') \rightarrow \textbf{let } n'' = inc\ n' \textbf{ in } \underline{S(n'')}$$

For example, $inc\ (S(S(Z)))$ returns $S(S(S(Z)))$. Since *inc* is injective, the inverse function inc^{-1} exists. But the naïve general inverse interpretation of *inc* has local *nondeterminism*; the underlined expressions can match the same value, $S(Z)$, and inverse interpretation cannot immediately distinguish between the branches.

A reversible functional languages must guarantee both backward determinism and termination (if the input for a given output exists) without using the general approach. Here, we propose a reversible functional language which has these properties. We say that a reversible language has *locally* forward and backward deterministic semantics. Below, we specify what this means in operational semantics.

For exploring the theoretical foundations of reversible computing, we focus on a purely-reversible and side-effect free first-order functional language. There exist several imperative and pseudo-functional reversible languages. As far as we know, Janus [12,20] is the first reversible language, and is imperative. We regard Gries' invertible language [11], R and PISA [8] as also belonging to this category. Baker proposed Ψ-Lisp [4], reversible linear Lisp; due to the use of a state and a hidden history stack, it is neither purely reversible nor purely functional. Mu, Hu, and Takeichi proposed INV [16], a point-free functional language with relational semantics, which essentially includes both forward and backward nondeterminism. Bowman, James, and Sabry have proposed Π [6], another point-free reversible functional language. Because of the nature of point-free languages, these do not have powerful pattern matching, so *e.g.* overlapping branch patterns in loops is prohibited. While the above examples all have reversible language features, a main contribution here is to separate reversibility in functional languages from other features.

Grammar: Syntax domains:

q $::=$ d^* (program) q $\in$ Programs
d $::=$ $f\ l \triangleq e$ (definition) d $\in$ Definitions
l $::=$ x (variable) f $\in$ Functions
   $|$ $c(l_1, \ldots, l_n)$ (constructor) l $\in$ Left-expressions
   $|$ $\lfloor l \rfloor$ (duplication/equality) e $\in$ Expressions
e $::=$ l (left-expression) x $\in$ Variables
   $|$ **let** $l_{out} = f\ l_{in}$ **in** e (let-expression) c $\in$ Constructors
   $|$ **rlet** $l_{in} = f\ l_{out}$ **in** e (rlet-expression)
   $|$ **case** l **of** $\{l_i \to e_i\}_{i=1}^m$ (case-expression)

Fig. 1. Abstract syntax of the first-order functional language ($n \geq 0$, $m \geq 1$)

2   The Language

The reversible functional language that we present here is simple, yet powerful enough to be r-Turing complete (see Section 2.6). Both in syntax and semantics, this language differs from conventional first-order functional languages. For example, the language is extended to include inverse function calls, and symmetric matching for case-expressions serves to make its semantics forward and backward deterministic. It may serve as a model for designing other, more sophisticated reversible functional languages.

2.1   Syntax

The first-order functional language (Fig. 1) is tailored to guarantee reversibility and is a modfied version of a language that was originally defined to investigate automatic program inversion [10]. A *program* q is a sequence of function definitions. A *function definition* d consists of a pattern l (left-expression) and a body e (expression). A *left-expression* l can contain variables, constructors and duplication/equality operators ($\lfloor \cdot \rfloor$). An expression e is a left-, let-, rlet- or case-expression. An *rlet-expression* invokes the inverse semantics of a function f. We call $l_i \to e_i$ the i-th *branch* of a case-expression.

We consider only well-formed programs in the following sense: each variable in patterns appears at most once, and each variable is bound before its use and is used *linearly* in each branch. A value v is recursively defined by a constructor c with arguments v_i: $v ::= c(v_1, \ldots, v_n)$ where $n \geq 0$. As is customary, a nullary constructor $c()$ is written as c. A list is constructed by an infix constructor (:) and a nullary constructor [] that represents the empty list. The unary and binary tuples, $\langle \cdot \rangle$ and $\langle \cdot, \cdot \rangle$, are a convenient shorthand for two different constructors.

2.2 Reversibility and Most General Matcher

Linearity is essential to a reversible language to avoid discarding values. Every variable defined by a pattern on the left-hand side of a case-expression must be used once in the expression on the right-hand side, otherwise information is lost.

Sometimes, we want to use a value more than once, but this is not allowed by linearity. Instead of duplicating the value implicitly by using a variable twice, we make this operation explicit by requiring that the value is duplicated by the operator $\lfloor \cdot \rfloor$. For example, rather than syntactically using variable h twice to duplicate the head of a list, as in expression $h : h : t$, the value is duplicated by $\lfloor \langle h \rangle \rfloor$ and bound to two fresh variables h_1 and h_2 in a case-expression:

Invalid

$dbl\ x \triangleq$ **case** x **of**
$\qquad h : t \to h : h : t$

Well-formed

$dbl\ x \triangleq$ **case** x **of**
$\qquad h : t \to$ **case** $\lfloor \langle h \rangle \rfloor$ **of**
$\qquad\qquad\qquad \langle h_1, h_2 \rangle \to h_1 : h_2 : t$

(2)

Using an explicit duplication operator simplifies the inversion of functional programs because duplication in one computation direction requires an equality test in the other direction, and vice versa.

The above *duplication/equality operator* [9] is defined by

$$\lfloor \langle v \rangle \rfloor = \langle v, v \rangle \qquad\qquad \text{(duplication)} \qquad (3)$$

$$\lfloor \langle v, v' \rangle \rfloor = \begin{cases} \langle v \rangle & \textbf{if } v = v' \\ \langle v, v' \rangle & \textbf{otherwise} \end{cases} \qquad \text{(equality test)} \qquad (4)$$

The operator is *self-inverse*, which means that it can be used to determine its input from its output (e.g., $\lfloor \langle v \rangle \rfloor = \langle v, v \rangle$ and $\langle v \rangle = \lfloor \langle v, v \rangle \rfloor$).

We take this idea further and allow the operator to occur also in the patterns of case-expressions. This simplifies forward and backward computation, and the inversion of programs. To illustrate this symmetry, consider the following pair-wise functionally equivalent case-expressions for duplicating and testing values:

case $\lfloor \langle l \rangle \rfloor$ **of**
$\qquad \langle x, y \rangle \to \cdots$

case $\langle l \rangle$ **of**
$\qquad \lfloor \langle x, y \rangle \rfloor \to \cdots$

(duplication) (5)

case $\lfloor \langle l, l' \rangle \rfloor$ **of**
$\qquad \langle x \rangle \to \cdots$
$\qquad \langle x, y \rangle \to \cdots$

case $\langle l, l' \rangle$ **of**
$\qquad \lfloor \langle x \rangle \rfloor \to \cdots$
$\qquad \lfloor \langle x, y \rangle \rfloor \to \cdots$

(equality test) (6)

This extension of patterns has the advantage that the same left-expressions can be used everywhere, which simplifies inverse computation and program inversion.

The $\lfloor \cdot \rfloor$-operator can occur anywhere in a left-expression (see Fig. 1). Equality of values in pairs can be tested at the leaf left-expressions in backward computation, which is useful for case selections, as we shall see in the example function

$$\frac{}{v \triangleleft x \rightsquigarrow \{x \mapsto v\}} \text{ VAR}$$

$$\frac{v_1 \triangleleft l_1 \rightsquigarrow \sigma_1 \quad \cdots \quad v_n \triangleleft l_n \rightsquigarrow \sigma_n}{c(v_1, \ldots, v_n) \triangleleft c(l_1, \ldots, l_n) \rightsquigarrow \biguplus_{i=1}^n \sigma_i} \text{ CON}$$

$$\frac{\lfloor v \rfloor \downarrow = v' \quad v' \triangleleft l \rightsquigarrow \sigma}{v \triangleleft \lfloor l \rfloor \rightsquigarrow \sigma} \text{ DUP/EQ}$$

Fig. 2. R-MATCH: Reversible matching operation ($\uplus$ denotes disjoint union)

plus (Fig. 4). Left-expressions define a unique composition and decomposition of values in our language. Pattern matching using left-expressions is formalized as follows. To define a reversible matching semantics, we use a *most general matcher* between left-expressions and values. Given linear left-expression l and value v, *left-exp judgment*

$$v \triangleleft l \rightsquigarrow \sigma \tag{7}$$

returns σ, the most general matcher of l and v. Figure 2 shows the semantic rules R-MATCH that define the most general matcher. A *substitution* σ is a mapping of variables x_i to values v_i: $\{x_1 \mapsto v_1, \ldots, x_n \mapsto v_n\}$ where $n \geq 0$. In particular, $\{\}$ is the identity substitution, σl is the application of σ to l, and $l \downarrow$ is the application of all $\lfloor \cdot \rfloor$-operators in left-expression l by means of Eq. 3 and 4.

Lemma 1 (The Most General Matcher). *Given value v and left-expression l, if left-exp judgment $v \triangleleft l \rightsquigarrow \sigma$ is satisfied, then σ is the most general matcher of l and v such that*

$$v \triangleleft l \rightsquigarrow \sigma \implies (\sigma l)\downarrow = v \land \forall \sigma'. \left[(\sigma' l)\downarrow = v \implies \exists \sigma''. \sigma' = \sigma \uplus \sigma'' \right]. \tag{8}$$

Proof. By straightforward induction on the derivation of $v \triangleleft l \rightsquigarrow \sigma$. □

2.3 Semantics

An *expression judgment* is a relation of a substitution σ, program q, expression e, and value v:

$$\sigma \vdash_q e \hookrightarrow v. \tag{9}$$

The operational semantics is defined in Fig. 3. LEFTEXP rule is resolved by a left-exp judgment. Without loss of generality, to avoid name clashes, we assume that l_f and e_f in the FUNEXP rule contain fresh variables each time f is applied.

LETEXP and RLETEXP rules have inverse functionality. While both rules apply function f in the premise, their input and output, as indicated by the subscripts, are exchanged. The reversible semantics allows us to define the inverse functionality by swapping the input and output without invoking program inversion. Only a reversible semantics enables this *rule sharing*. We shall see examples of rlet-expressions later when we define a reversible Turing machine.

The CASEEXP rule is more involved. We constrain the semantics of case-expressions to be symmetric regarding the branch selection by requiring that the

$$\frac{v \lhd l \rightsquigarrow \sigma}{\sigma \vdash_q l \hookrightarrow v} \text{ LeftExp}$$

$$\frac{f \ l_f \triangleq e_f \in q \quad \sigma \vdash_q l \hookrightarrow v' \quad v' \lhd l_f \rightsquigarrow \sigma_f \quad \sigma_f \vdash_q e_f \hookrightarrow v}{\sigma \vdash_q f \ l \hookrightarrow v} \text{ FunExp}$$

$$\frac{\sigma_{in} \vdash_q f \ l_{in} \hookrightarrow v_{out} \quad v_{out} \lhd l_{out} \rightsquigarrow \sigma_{out} \quad \sigma_{out} \uplus \sigma_e \vdash_q e \hookrightarrow v}{\sigma_{in} \uplus \sigma_e \vdash_q \textbf{let } l_{out} = f \ l_{in} \textbf{ in } e \hookrightarrow v} \text{ LetExp}$$

$$\frac{v_{in} \lhd l_{in} \rightsquigarrow \sigma_{in} \quad \sigma_{out} \vdash_q f \ l_{out} \hookrightarrow v_{in} \quad \sigma_{out} \uplus \sigma_e \vdash_q e \hookrightarrow v}{\sigma_{in} \uplus \sigma_e \vdash_q \textbf{rlet } l_{in} = f \ l_{out} \textbf{ in } e \hookrightarrow v} \text{ RLetExp}$$

$$\frac{\sigma_l \vdash_q l \hookrightarrow v' \quad \sigma_{l_j} \uplus \sigma_t \vdash_q e_j \hookrightarrow v}{j = \min\{i \mid v' \lhd l_i \rightsquigarrow \sigma_{l_i}\} = \min\{i \mid l' \in leaves(e_i) \wedge v \lhd l' \rightsquigarrow \_\}}{\sigma_l \uplus \sigma_t \vdash_q \textbf{case } l \textbf{ of } \{l_i \rightarrow e_i\}_{i=1}^m \hookrightarrow v} \text{ CaseExp}$$

Fig. 3. Operational semantics for the reversible functional language

first-matching branch is the same in *both* directions. Otherwise, the CaseExp is undefined. Consider the following case-expression as an example.

$$\textbf{case } l \textbf{ of}$$
$$l_1 \rightarrow \ \cdots \ \textbf{in } l'_1$$
$$\vdots$$
$$l_i \rightarrow \ \cdots \ \textbf{in } l'_i \tag{10}$$
$$\vdots$$
$$l_n \rightarrow \ \cdots \ \textbf{in } l'_n$$

The value v of l is matched against the left-hand side of each branch (l_1, l_2, ...) until the first successful match at some l_i, that is, $v \lhd l_i \rightsquigarrow \sigma_i$. As usual, the right-hand side of the i-th branch is then evaluated in σ_i and a value v' is returned by l'_i. Now, for symmetry, we require that v' does *not* match any of the preceding $l'_1, \ldots, l'_{i-1}$; otherwise, the case-expression is undefined. This *symmetric first-match policy* ensures that case-expressions forward and backward deterministic.

Thus, in backward computation, a given value v' of the whole case-expression is matched against the leaf left-expressions of each branch (l'_1, l'_2, ...) until the first successful match at some l'_i, that is, $v' \lhd l'_i \rightsquigarrow \sigma'_i$. The result of the backward computation of the right hand side of the i-th branch instantiates l_i to v. Then, for symmetry, we require that v does not match any of the preceding $l_1, \ldots, l_{i-1}$; otherwise, evaluating the case-expression is undefined. (The set *leaves*(e) contains all left-expressions at the tips of e.[1]) Therefore, as usual, $l_1, \ldots, l_n$ need not be syntactically orthogonal and the same holds for $l'_1, \ldots, l'_n$.

---

[1] *leaves*($\textbf{let } l_1 = f \ l_2 \textbf{ in } e$)=*leaves*($e$), *leaves*($\textbf{case } l \textbf{ of } \{p_i \rightarrow e_i\}_{i=1}^m$) = $\cup_{i=1}^m leaves(e_i)$
leaves($\textbf{rlet } l_1 = f \ l_2 \textbf{ in } e$) = *leaves*($e$), *leaves*($l$) = $\{l\}$.

$$
\begin{aligned}
\textit{fib } n \triangleq \textbf{ case } n \textbf{ of} \\
Z \quad &\to \langle S(Z), S(Z) \rangle \\
S(m) &\to \textbf{let } \langle x, y \rangle = \textit{fib } m \textbf{ in} \\
&\quad \textbf{let } z = \textit{plus } \langle y, x \rangle \textbf{ in } z
\end{aligned}
\tag{12}
$$

$$
\begin{aligned}
\textit{plus } \langle x, y \rangle \triangleq \textbf{ case } y \textbf{ of} \\
Z \quad &\to \lfloor \langle x \rangle \rfloor \\
S(u) &\to \textbf{let } \langle x', u' \rangle = \textit{plus } \langle x, u \rangle \textbf{ in } \langle x', S(u') \rangle
\end{aligned}
\tag{13}
$$

Fig. 4. Fibonacci-pair function $\textit{fib}$ and addition $\textit{plus}\langle x, y \rangle = \langle x, x + y \rangle$[2]

Because of the symmetric semantics of case-expressions, we can compute the increment function from above both forward and backward:

$$
\{n \mapsto Z\} \vdash_q \textit{inc } n \hookrightarrow S(Z)
\tag{11}
$$

where q is a program which includes the function definition of $\textit{inc}$ in Eq. 1. Without the symmetric first-match policy, the value $S(Z)$ could be a consequence of two different instances of the CASEEXP rule because $S(Z)$ matches both of the underlined left-expressions $S(Z)$ and $S(n'')$, and we would thus have to search deeper in the derivation tree to decide which was the right instance. However, the policy ensures that inverse interpretation is locally deterministic and, in this example, selects the first branch and never the second.

If a function terminates with an output for a given input, inverse computation of the function terminates for that output and returns the original input, and vice versa.

Example program. Given a number n, the *Fibonacci-pair function* [9] computes a tuple containing the $(n + 1)$-th and $(n + 2)$-th Fibonacci number. The functions $\textit{fib}$ and $\textit{plus}$ are defined for Peano numbers in Fig. 4. Note the use of the $\lfloor \cdot \rfloor$-operator on the right-hand side of the first branch of $\textit{plus}$ to duplicate x in forward computation and to check equality of a pair of values in backward computation. We can relate numbers to the corresponding Fibonacci pairs via an expression judgment. For example, for the second pair we have:

$$
\{n \mapsto S(S(Z))\} \vdash_q \textit{fib } n \hookrightarrow \langle S(S(Z)), S(S(S(Z))) \rangle
\tag{14}
$$

2.4 Reversibility and Semantics

In this section, we show in what sense the functional language defined above is reversible. We first examine the matching operation (left-expression judgments) and then continue with the rules of the operational semantics (expression judgments).

---

[2] For simplicity, $x + y$ represents the Peano number for the sum of x and y.

We have local determinism in the left-exp judgment in the sense that l determines uniquely which rule applies, and in the premises each left-expression is uniquely determined. Here, let _ be a wildcard value or a wildcard substitution.[3]

Lemma 2 (The Unique Derivation of Left-Exp Judgments ($\cdot \lhd l \rightsquigarrow \cdot$)).
Any left-exp judgment $\_ \lhd l \rightsquigarrow \_$ is the consequence of at most a single rule in Fig. 2 and in its premises left-expressions are determined uniquely.

Proof. Given linear left-expression l, left-exp judgment $\_ \lhd l \rightsquigarrow \_$ determines which rule to apply because all left-expressions l in the consequences are orthogonal. Also, all and only the immediate proper sub-left-expressions of l (*e.g.* $l_1, \ldots, l_n$ for $l = c(l_1, \ldots, l_n)$) appear exactly once in the premise left-exp judgments, which are thus also determined uniquely. □

This implies efficiency for an implementation of the left-exp judgment, as the structure of l completely decides the structure of the derivation. We further have that for any given left-expression l the left-exp judgment is an injective relation between substitutions and values.

Lemma 3 (The Global Reversibility of Left-Exp Judgments ($\cdot \lhd l \rightsquigarrow \cdot$)).
The R-MATCH relation $\cdot \lhd \cdot \rightsquigarrow \cdot$ (Fig. 2) obeys the following formulas.

$$\forall l \forall \sigma \forall v_1 \forall v_2.\ v_1 \lhd l \rightsquigarrow \sigma \ \wedge\ v_2 \lhd l \rightsquigarrow \sigma \implies v_1 = v_2 \tag{15}$$

$$\forall l \forall v \forall \sigma_1 \forall \sigma_2.\ v \lhd l \rightsquigarrow \sigma_1 \ \wedge\ v \lhd l \rightsquigarrow \sigma_2 \implies \sigma_1 = \sigma_2 \tag{16}$$

Proof. By Lemma 2 the derivation tree for any left-expression judgment completely and uniquely follows the structure of l, so the two derivations in the antecedents of the implications in formulas (15) and (16) must use the same rules in both consequence and premises. By induction on these derivations the lemma then easily follows. □

Note that Lemma 2 does not imply Lemma 3 for arbitrary rule sets, and that the inverse direction is also not satisfied: it is possible to satisfy global reversibility without unique derivations. Also, the rule set in which the VAR rule is replaced with

$$\frac{}{\_ \lhd x \rightsquigarrow \{x \mapsto \_\}} \text{VAR'}$$

still satisfies Lemma 2 but not Lemma 3.

In the operational semantics (Fig. 3) for the exp-judgment, we again have that the rule selection is locally and uniquely determined.

Lemma 4 (The Unique Derivation of Exp-Judgments ($\cdot \vdash_q e \hookrightarrow \cdot$)).
Any expression judgment $\_ \vdash_q e \hookrightarrow \_$ is the consequence of at most a single rule in Fig. 3 and in its premises expressions and left-expressions are determined uniquely, except for the CASEEXP rule where either a substitution σ or value v is needed for uniqueness.

---

[3] The instances of a wildcard value are arbitrary; two wildcards do not necessarily have the same value.

Proof. Analogous to Lemma 2, expression e uniquely determines which rule to apply because all expressions e in the consequences are orthogonal. For all rules except CASEEXP the syntactic form of the expression in the consequence of the exp-judgment also determines which rules to apply in the premises by simple case analysis.

In the CASEEXP rule, the symmetric first-match policy determines the premise for the case chosen, so the value of j depends on the particular substitution σ (or value v), meaning that e_j is not syntactically defined by e alone (as all the other expressions and left-expressions in the premises are). However, for a given substitution σ (or value v) uniqueness of e_j follows by Lemmas 2 and 3.   □

This sort of *local determinism* and the reversibility of left-exp judgments leads to the following lemma.

Lemma 5 (The Global Reversibility of Exp-Judgments $(\cdot \vdash_q e \hookrightarrow \cdot)$).
The operational semantics $(\cdot \vdash_q \cdot \hookrightarrow \cdot)$ (Fig. 3) obeys the following formulas.

$$\forall e \forall v \forall \sigma_1 \forall \sigma_2.\ \sigma_1 \vdash_q e \hookrightarrow v\ \wedge\ \sigma_2 \vdash_q e \hookrightarrow v \implies \sigma_1 = \sigma_2 \qquad (17)$$

$$\forall e \forall \sigma \forall v_1 \forall v_2.\ \sigma \vdash_q e \hookrightarrow v_1\ \wedge\ \sigma \vdash_q e \hookrightarrow v_2 \implies v_1 = v_2 \qquad (18)$$

Proof (Sketch). Similar to Lemma 3, by induction on the derivations of the exp-judgments in the antecedent of each implication. The reversibility of any left-exp judgments in the premises of such derivations is ensured by Lemma 3.   □

While property (18) should be recognizable as forward determinism, the reversibility of the language semantics is encapsulated by property (17) and is distinctly non-standard: for any given expression e (including functional calls), we only need the resulting value v, to determine the unique initial environment σ wherein e evaluates to v.

Analogous to the relationship between Lemma 2 and Lemma 3, Lemma 4 does not imply Lemma 5 and the inverse direction is also not satisfied.

Reversibility affects termination analysis as well. Reversibility guarantees that backward interpretation terminates if forward interpretation terminates, and vice versa. On the other hand, reversibility does not by itself guarantee termination. Consider the function

$$\textit{infinite } x\ \triangleq\ \textbf{let } y = \textit{infinite } x \textbf{ in } y. \qquad (19)$$

For example, we can reasonably expect that in an implementation, the function expression *infinite Z* is recursively unfolded arbitrary times by the LETEXP and FUNEXP rules, leading to non-termination. However, the infinite unfolding process is still locally reversible and the expression (vacuously) satisfies the global reversibility properties described in Lemma 5.

2.5   Examples

We shall here show how programs are realized in the proposed language, and how program inversion is lightweight. *Run-length encoding* is a data compression

$$pack\ s \triangleq \textbf{case}\ s\ \textbf{of}$$
$$[] \quad \rightarrow []$$
$$c_1 : r \rightarrow \textbf{let}\ s = pack\ r\ \textbf{in}$$
$$\textbf{case}\ s\ \textbf{of}$$
$$[] \quad \rightarrow \langle c_1, S(Z) \rangle : []$$
$$h : t \rightarrow \textbf{case}\ h\ \textbf{of}$$
$$\langle c_2, n \rangle \rightarrow \textbf{case}\ \lfloor \langle c_1, c_2 \rangle \rfloor\ \textbf{of}$$
$$\langle c_1', c_2' \rangle \rightarrow \langle c_1', S(Z) \rangle : (\langle c_2', n \rangle : t)$$
$$\langle c \rangle \quad \rightarrow \langle c, S(n) \rangle : t$$
$$(20)$$

Fig. 5. Run-length encoding function *pack*

algorithm in which each contiguous single-character sequence is replaced with a pair of the character and its count. In the proposed reversible language a (recursive) program for run-length encoding *pack* is shown in Fig. 5 (cf. [9]). For example, $pack\ [A, A, B, C, C, C]$[4] evaluates to $[\langle A, 2 \rangle, \langle B, 1 \rangle, \langle C, 3 \rangle]$,[5] which is realized by an expression judgment

$$\{ \}\vdash_q pack\ [A, A, B, C, C, C] \hookrightarrow [\langle A, 2 \rangle, \langle B, 1 \rangle, \langle C, 3 \rangle]. \quad (21)$$

Now, all functions are reversible, and can be inversely applied. Hence, function *unpack* can be defined very simply using *pack*:

$$unpack\ x \triangleq \textbf{rlet}\ x = pack\ y\ \textbf{in}\ y. \quad (22)$$

In general, for any well-formed function f and variables x and y, expression

$$\textbf{rlet}\ x = f\ y\ \textbf{in}\ y \quad (23)$$

returns the same value as $f^{-1}\ x$ does where f^{-1} is an inverse function of f.

In contrast to irreversible languages, program inversion for the reversible language is always possible and lightweight in the sense that it does not require global program analysis. A recursive descent local program inversion for the language is given in Fig. 6. For the inversion of case expression, unification of left-expression l and each of the patterns p_i is used to generate patterns for the inverse cases. Failure of unification means that the branch is never selected no matter what instances of l are provided in the forward interpretation. Even in such a case, the translation of the branch e_i has to continue, as the symmetric first-match policy enforces us to check the tips of e_i during computation.

For example, program inversion of *fib* in Fig. 4 yields fib^{-1} in Fig. 7. As in an ordinary functional language, the first-match policy in the forward direction

---

[4] Following the standard convention, list $A : B : C : []$ is abbreviated as $[A, B, C]$.

[5] For brevity, Peano numbers are here represented by ordinary decimal numbers.

$$\mathcal{I}_p[\![d^*]\!] \;=\; \mathcal{I}_d[\![d]\!]^*$$

$$\mathcal{I}_d[\![f\; l \triangleq e]\!] \;=\; f^{-1}\; x \triangleq \mathbf{case}\; x\; \mathbf{of}\; \mathcal{I}[\![e, l]\!]$$

$$\mathcal{I}[\![l, e]\!] \;=\; \{l \to e\}$$

$$\mathcal{I}[\![\mathbf{let}\; l_1 \;=\; f\; l_2 \;\mathbf{in}\; e', e]\!] \;=\; \mathcal{I}[\![e', \mathbf{let}\; l_2 = f^{-1}\; l_1\; \mathbf{in}\; e]\!]$$

$$\mathcal{I}[\![\mathbf{rlet}\; l_1 \;=\; f\; l_2 \;\mathbf{in}\; e', e]\!] \;=\; \mathcal{I}[\![e', \mathbf{rlet}\; l_2 = f^{-1}\; l_1\; \mathbf{in}\; e]\!]$$

$$\mathcal{I}[\![\mathbf{case}\; l\; \mathbf{of}\; \{p_i \to e_i\}_{i=1}^m, e]\!] \;=\; \cup_{i=1}^m(\mathbf{if}\; \sigma_i \neq \bot\; \mathbf{then}\; \mathcal{I}[\![e_i, \sigma_i e]\!]$$

$$\mathbf{else}\; \mathcal{I}[\![e_i, \mathbf{case}\; p_i\; \mathbf{of}\; l \to e]\!])$$

$$\mathbf{where}\; \sigma_i\; \text{is the unification of}\; l\; \text{and}\; p_i$$

Fig. 6. Program inversion (x is a fresh variable)

$$
\begin{aligned}
\mathit{fib}^{-1}\; x_1 \;\triangleq\; &\mathbf{case}\; x_1\; \mathbf{of}\\
&\langle S(Z), S(Z)\rangle \to Z\\
&x_2 \qquad\qquad\; \to \mathbf{let}\; \langle y, x\rangle = \mathit{plus}^{-1}\; x_2\; \mathbf{in}\\
&\qquad\qquad\qquad\quad \mathbf{let}\; m = \mathit{fib}^{-1}\; \langle x, y\rangle\; \mathbf{in}\\
&\qquad\qquad\qquad\quad S(m)
\end{aligned}
\tag{24}
$$

$$
\begin{aligned}
\mathit{plus}^{-1}\; z \;\triangleq\; &\mathbf{case}\; z\; \mathbf{of}\\
&\lfloor\langle x\rangle\rfloor \qquad\; \to \langle x, Z\rangle\\
&\langle x', S(u')\rangle \to \mathbf{let}\; \langle x, u\rangle = \mathit{plus}^{-1}\; \langle x', u'\rangle\; \mathbf{in}\; \langle x, S(u)\rangle
\end{aligned}
\tag{25}
$$

Fig. 7. Inverse functions of *fib* and *plus* (x_1 and x_2 are fresh variables)

ensures x_2 only match with values that are not $\langle S(Z), S(Z)\rangle$. The subtraction, $\mathit{plus}^{-1}\langle x, x + y\rangle = \langle x, y\rangle$, is obtained by program inversion of *plus* from Fig. 4. Here, we see how it is convenient that the $\lfloor \cdot \rfloor$ operator can occur in the pattern of a case-expression, so that, in this example, the inversion is realized by just swapping the left- and right-hand sides of branches.

2.6   *r*-Turing Completeness

We show the proposed language is r-Turing complete [3]; the language can simulate any reversible Turing machine (RTM).

Definition 1 (Turing Machine). *A Turing machine T is a tuple $(Q, \Sigma, b, \delta, q_s, q_f)$ where Q is a finite set of states, Σ is a finite set of tape symbols, $b \in \Sigma$ is the blank symbol,*

$$\delta : Q \times [(\Sigma \times \Sigma) \cup \{\leftarrow, \downarrow, \rightarrow\}] \times Q \tag{26}$$

is a partial relation defining the transition rules, $q_s \in Q$ is the starting state, and $q_f \in Q$ is the final state. Symbols $\leftarrow, \downarrow, \rightarrow$ represent the three shift directions (left, stay, right).

The form of a triple $\in \delta$ is either $\langle q_1, \langle s_1, s_2 \rangle, q_2 \rangle$ or $\langle q_1, d, q_2 \rangle$ where $q_1, q_2 \in Q$, $s_1, s_2 \in \Sigma$, and $d \in \{\leftarrow, \downarrow, \rightarrow\}$. The former *symbol rule* says that in state q_1 with the tape head reading symbol s_1, write s_2 and change into state q_2. The latter *shift rule* says that in state q_1, move the tape head in direction d and change the state to q_2.

Definition 2 (Reversible Turing Machine [5,3]). *A Turing machine T is* forward deterministic *iff for any distinct pair of triples $\langle q_1, a, q_2 \rangle \in \delta$ and $\langle q_1', a', q_2' \rangle \in \delta$, if $q_1 = q_1'$ then $a = \langle s_1, s_2 \rangle \wedge a' = \langle s_1', s_2' \rangle \wedge s_1 \neq s_2$. A Turing machine is* backward deterministic *iff for any distinct pair of triples $\langle q_1, a, q_2 \rangle \in \delta$ and $\langle q_1', a', q_2' \rangle \in \delta$, if $q_2 = q_2'$ then $a = \langle s_1, s_2 \rangle \wedge a' = \langle s_1', s_2' \rangle \wedge s_2 \neq s_2'$. A Turing machine is* reversible *iff it is forward and backward deterministic.*

If the number of non-blank symbols on the tape is finite, the infinite length tape can be uniquely represented by a triple $\langle l, s, r \rangle$ where l and r hold the left and right non-blank portions of the tape (in the form of lists) with respect to the tape head, and s contains the symbol under the tape head. To realize an infinite tape in finite space in the reversible setting, we require that only non-blank symbols can be on the bottom of either tape stack, cf. [18].

Let *step* be an implementation of the transition relation, such that *step* takes a configuration (a pair of the current state and tape) and returns the next configuration. Given a sequence of state transition rules d^*, we obtain

$$step \ \langle q, t \rangle \ \triangleq \ \textbf{case} \ \langle q, t \rangle \ \textbf{of} \qquad (27)$$
$$\mathcal{T}[\![d]\!]^*$$

where $\mathcal{T}$ is a translator from a state transition rule to the corresponding case branch in the proposed language, defined as:

$$
\begin{aligned}
\mathcal{T}[\![\langle q_1, \langle s_1, s_2 \rangle, q_2 \rangle]\!] &= \langle \overline{q_1}, \langle l, \overline{s_1}, r \rangle \rangle \rightarrow \langle \overline{q_2}, \langle l, \overline{s_2}, r \rangle \rangle \\
\mathcal{T}[\![\langle q_1, \leftarrow, q_2 \rangle]\!] &= \langle \overline{q_1}, t' \rangle \rightarrow \textbf{let } t' = move_l \ t'' \ \textbf{in} \ \langle \overline{q_2}, t'' \rangle \\
\mathcal{T}[\![\langle q_1, \rightarrow, q_2 \rangle]\!] &= \langle \overline{q_1}, t' \rangle \rightarrow \textbf{rlet } t'' = move_l \ t' \ \textbf{in} \ \langle \overline{q_2}, t'' \rangle \\
\mathcal{T}[\![\langle q_1, \downarrow, q_2 \rangle]\!] &= \langle \overline{q_1}, t' \rangle \rightarrow \langle \overline{q_2}, t' \rangle
\end{aligned} \qquad (28)
$$

An overlined state or symbol $\overline{\cdot}$ represents a corresponding constructor in the language. Because of the reversibility of the source RTM, leaf left-expressions as well as the patterns appearing in the branches of *step* are disjoint, leading to the reversibility of *step*.

As an example, consider the incrementation of a non-negative binary number yielding its successor in binary representation (with the least significant digit first), cf. [18]. An RTM computing this function is shown in Fig. 8. It works as follows: Initially, the tape head is to the left of the first bit. The tape head then moves to the right, flipping bits until it flips a 0 to a 1, and then returns to the original position. It is easily verified that the machine in Fig. 8 is reversible. The rules given in Fig. 8 are translated into function *step* in Fig. 9.

$$\langle q_s, \langle b, b \rangle, q_1 \rangle \qquad \langle q_2, \langle 0, 1 \rangle, q_3 \rangle \qquad \langle q_2, \langle b, b \rangle, q_3 \rangle \qquad \langle q_4, \langle 0, 0 \rangle, q_3 \rangle$$
$$\langle q_1, \rightarrow, q_2 \rangle \qquad \langle q_2, \langle 1, 0 \rangle, q_1 \rangle \qquad \langle q_3, \leftarrow, q_4 \rangle \qquad \langle q_4, \langle b, b \rangle, q_f \rangle$$

Fig. 8. Transition rules for binary number incrementation

$$
\begin{aligned}
step \ \langle q, t \rangle \ &\triangleq \ \mathbf{case} \ \langle q, t \rangle \ \mathbf{of} \\
&\langle \overline{q_s}, \langle l, \overline{b}, r \rangle \rangle \rightarrow \langle \overline{q_1}, \langle l, \overline{b}, r \rangle \rangle \\
&\langle \overline{q_1}, t' \rangle \qquad \rightarrow \mathbf{rlet} \ t' = move_l \ t'' \ \mathbf{in} \ \langle \overline{q_2}, t'' \rangle \\
&\langle \overline{q_2}, \langle l, \overline{0}, r \rangle \rangle \rightarrow \langle \overline{q_3}, \langle l, \overline{1}, r \rangle \rangle \\
&\langle \overline{q_2}, \langle l, \overline{1}, r \rangle \rangle \rightarrow \langle \overline{q_1}, \langle l, \overline{0}, r \rangle \rangle \\
&\langle \overline{q_2}, \langle l, \overline{b}, r \rangle \rangle \rightarrow \langle \overline{q_3}, \langle l, \overline{b}, r \rangle \rangle \\
&\langle \overline{q_3}, t' \rangle \qquad \rightarrow \mathbf{let} \ t'' = move_l \ t' \ \mathbf{in} \ \langle \overline{q_4}, t'' \rangle \\
&\langle \overline{q_4}, \langle l, \overline{0}, r \rangle \rangle \rightarrow \langle \overline{q_3}, \langle l, \overline{0}, r \rangle \rangle \\
&\langle \overline{q_4}, \langle l, \overline{b}, r \rangle \rangle \rightarrow \langle \overline{q_f}, \langle l, \overline{b}, r \rangle \rangle
\end{aligned}
$$

Fig. 9. Function *step* generated from the transition rules in Fig. 8

Function $move_l$ moves the tape head one cell to the left. Thus, when it is called in an **rlet**-expression, it moves the tape head to the right. Function $move_l$ is defined as:

$$
\begin{aligned}
move_l \ \langle l, s, r \rangle \ &\triangleq \ \mathbf{let} \ r' = pushtape \ \langle s, r \rangle \ \mathbf{in} \\
&\quad \mathbf{rlet} \ l = pushtape \ \langle s', l' \rangle \ \mathbf{in} \\
&\quad \langle l', s', r' \rangle
\end{aligned}
\tag{29}
$$

where $pushtape \ \langle s, stk \rangle$ pushes symbol s to stack (list) stk:

$$
\begin{aligned}
pushtape \ \langle s, stk \rangle \ &\triangleq \ \mathbf{case} \ \langle s, stk \rangle \ \mathbf{of} \\
&\langle \overline{b}, [\,] \rangle \rightarrow [\,] \\
&\langle s', tl \rangle \rightarrow s' : tl
\end{aligned}
\tag{30}
$$

When symbol s is a blank and stack stk is empty, *pushtape* leaves stk empty. Otherwise, s is pushed on stk. Conversely, when *pushtape* is inversely invoked with an empty stack, a blank symbol is popped. This operation can be repeated arbitrary times. This preserves the condition that the bottom element of a stack is non-blank, which enables the representation of the infinite length tape in reversible finite space.

To simulate the RTM we must apply *step* repeatedly until we reach the final state q_f. If this is naïvely implemented, it results in a many-to-one (non-invertible) mapping which is not a reversible function. To cope with this problem we add an extra (intermediate) element to the output. For an RTM running forward, in addition to the result we also return a natural number which counts the number of applications of *step*. A simulation of the RTM is defined by the function rtm_f. Given a pair of the state and tape $\langle q, t \rangle$, rtm_f returns a triple containing the state, tape, and counter.

$$
rtm_f \langle q, t \rangle \triangleq \textbf{case } q \textbf{ of} \\
\overline{q_f} \rightarrow \langle \overline{q_f}, t, Z \rangle \\
q_1 \rightarrow \textbf{let } \langle q_2, t_2 \rangle = step \langle q_1, t \rangle \textbf{ in} \\
\textbf{let } \langle q_3, t_3, n \rangle = rtm_f \langle q_2, t_2 \rangle \textbf{ in} \\
\langle q_3, t_3, S(n) \rangle
\tag{31}
$$

A simulation of the inverse RTM is similarly defined by rtm_b:

$$
rtm_b \langle q, t \rangle \triangleq \textbf{case } q \textbf{ of} \\
\overline{q_s} \rightarrow \langle \overline{q_s}, t, Z \rangle \\
q_1 \rightarrow \textbf{rlet } \langle q_1, t \rangle = step \langle q_2, t_2 \rangle \textbf{ in} \\
\textbf{let } \langle q_3, t_3, n \rangle = rtm_b \langle q_2, t_2 \rangle \textbf{ in} \\
\langle q_3, t_3, S(n) \rangle
\tag{32}
$$

Here, **rlet** allows us to access to the inverse semantics explicitly, so that function *step* is used in the backward direction. This unconventional *code sharing* is a unique feature of reversible languages. Seeing as the underlying RTM is the same, rtm_f and rtm_b will recurse exactly the same number of times when applied to an input and the corresponding output, respectively. Because of this we can apply a recent input-erasing reversible simulation which removes the garbage counters, and which is twice as fast as Bennett's general method [19]. In fact, we directly obtain the following optimized RTM simulation:

$$
rtm\ t \triangleq \textbf{case } \lfloor \langle t \rangle \rfloor \textbf{ of} \\
\langle t_1, t_2 \rangle \rightarrow \textbf{let } \langle \overline{q_f}, t_3, n \rangle = rtm_f \langle \overline{q_s}, t_1 \rangle \textbf{ in} \\
\textbf{rlet } \langle \overline{q_s}, t_2, n \rangle = rtm_b \langle \overline{q_f}, t_4 \rangle \textbf{ in} \\
\textbf{case } \lfloor \langle t_3, t_4 \rangle \rfloor \textbf{ of} \\
\langle t' \rangle \rightarrow t'
\tag{33}
$$

which is a function of tapes to tapes (without the counter) corresponding exactly to the RTM defined by *step*.

For any RTM the above translation is obviously possible, and so the language is r-Turing complete: it is a universal reversible language.

3 Conclusion

We proposed a simple first-order reversible functional language. We view reversibility as both *global and local determinism* in both execution directions, and specified corresponding properties for an operational semantics for the functional lanaguage. Reversibility is achieved by reversible matching and syntactic restrictions (including linearity of variables). Using a novel symmetric first-match policy for pattern matching, the backward semantics of the proposed language is deterministic even in the case of overlapping leaf left-expressions, which enables concise code. The proposed reversible functional language is universal, as powerful as reversible Turing machines.

Every reversible computation model, be it reversible Turing machines [5,3], reversible cellular automata [15], or reversible logic circuits [7,17], have their own languages to describe how computation is organized. It is our hope that this language can serve as a basis for further research on reversible computing in the functional setting, similar to how Janus is used in the imperative setting. For example, Janus has been used for partial evaluation of a reversible language [14], synthesizing reversible circuits [17, Chapter 3] and translation of reversible languages [2].

Acknowledgments. This work is in part supported by Nanzan University Pache Research Subsidy I-A-2 for the 2011 academic year.

References

1. Abramov, S.M., Glück, R.: Principles of Inverse Computation and the Universal Resolving Algorithm. In: Mogensen, T.Æ., Schmidt, D.A., Sudborough, I.H. (eds.) The Essence of Computation. LNCS, vol. 2566, pp. 269–295. Springer, Heidelberg (2002)
2. Axelsen, H.B.: Clean Translation of an Imperative Reversible Programming Language. In: Knoop, J. (ed.) CC 2011. LNCS, vol. 6601, pp. 144–163. Springer, Heidelberg (2011)
3. Axelsen, H.B., Glück, R.: What Do Reversible Programs Compute? In: Hofmann, M. (ed.) FOSSACS 2011. LNCS, vol. 6604, pp. 42–56. Springer, Heidelberg (2011)
4. Baker, H.G.: NREVERSAL of Fortune — The Thermodynamics of Garbage Collection. In: Bekkers, Y., Cohen, J. (eds.) IWMM 1992. LNCS, vol. 637, pp. 507–524. Springer, Heidelberg (1992)
5. Bennett, C.H.: Logical reversibility of computation. IBM Journal of Research and Development 17(6), 525–532 (1973)
6. Bowman, W.J., James, R.P., Sabry, A.: Dagger traced symmetric monoidal categories and reversible programming. In: De Vos, A., Wille, R. (eds.) 3rd Workshop on Reversible Computation, pp. 51–56. University of Gent. (2011)
7. De Vos, A.: Reversible Computing: Fundamentals, Quantum Computing, and Applications. Wiley-VCH (2010)
8. Frank, M.P.: Reversibility for efficient computing. Ph.D. thesis, EECS Dept. MIT, Cambridge, Massachusetts (1999)
9. Glück, R., Kawabe, M.: A Program Inverter for a Functional Language with Equality and Constructors. In: Ohori, A. (ed.) APLAS 2003. LNCS, vol. 2895, pp. 246–264. Springer, Heidelberg (2003)
10. Glück, R., Kawabe, M.: A method for automatic program inversion based on LR(0) parsing. Fundamenta Informaticae 66(4), 367–395 (2005)
11. Gries, D.: Inverting Programs. In: The Science of Programming. Texts and Monographs in Computer Science, ch. 21, pp. 265–274. Springer, Heidelberg (1981)
12. Lutz, C.: Janus: a time-reversible language. Letter to R. Landauer (1986), http://www.tetsuo.jp/ref/janus.html

13. McCarthy, J.: The inversion of functions defined by Turing machines. In: Shannon, C.E., McCarthy, J. (eds.) Automata Studies, pp. 177–181. Princeton University Press (1956)

14. Mogensen, T.Æ.: Partial evaluation of the reversible language Janus. In: Proceedings of Partial Evaluation and Program Manipulation, pp. 23–32. ACM Press (2011)

15. Morita, K.: Reversible computing and cellular automata — A survey. Theoretical Computer Science 395(1), 101–131 (2008)

16. Mu, S.C., Hu, Z., Takeichi, M.: An Injective Language for Reversible Computation. In: Kozen, D. (ed.) MPC 2004. LNCS, vol. 3125, pp. 289–313. Springer, Heidelberg (2004)

17. Wille, R., Drechsler, R.: Towards a Design Flow for Reversible Logic. Springer, Heidelberg (2010)

18. Yokoyama, T., Axelsen, H., Glück, R.: Principles of a reversible programming language. In: Proceedings of Computing Frontiers, pp. 43–54. ACM Press (2008)

19. Yokoyama, T., Axelsen, H.B., Glück, R.: Optimizing clean reversible simulation of injective functions. Journal of Multiple-Valued Logic and Soft Computing 18(1), 5–24 (2012)

20. Yokoyama, T., Glück, R.: A reversible programming language and its invertible self-interpreter. In: Proceedings of Partial Evaluation and Semantics-Based Program Manipulation, pp. 144–153. ACM Press (2007)

A Reversible Processor Architecture and Its Reversible Logic Design

Michael Kirkedal Thomsen, Holger Bock Axelsen, and Robert Glück

DIKU, Department of Computer Science, University of Copenhagen
Universitetsparken 1, DK-2100 Copenhagen, Denmark
{shapper,funkstar}@diku.dk, glueck@acm.org

Abstract. We describe the design of a purely reversible computing architecture, Bob, and its instruction set, BobISA. The special features of the design include a simple, yet expressive, locally-invertible instruction set, and fully reversible control logic and address calculation. We have designed an architecture with an ISA that is expressive enough to serve as the target for a compiler from a high-level structured reversible programming language.

All-in-all, this paper demonstrates that the design of a complete reversible computing architecture is possible and can serve as the core of a programmable reversible computing system.

1 Introduction

Energy consumption is an important aspect of most computing systems today and this is especially true for embedded systems and battery-dependent computers. Reversible computing has the potential to reduce power consumption and heat dissipation [11, 14].

The design of reversible computing systems and programs is, however, not a trivial extension of the conventional case. Not all problems have simple reversible implementations and rethinking the entire problem might be needed for a solution. Reversible programming languages [15, 28] have special constructs (*e.g.* an *if-then-else* statement also needs a joining *assertion* that verifies the computational path) which complicates program development, and the need for new programming methodologies is evident.

There are, however, specific domains that are clear-cut for reversible computing: lossless discrete transformations like FFT and wavelets [10] used in compression and analysis of multimedia signals, or simulation of physical systems. Developments in areas from low-level circuit design [9] and synthesis [16, 19, 25] to high-level languages such as Janus [27, 28] and compilers [1] have also provided more insight to the design of reversible systems.

Fully reversible computing systems[1] are still years of development away from general purpose computers. In this paper we show the design of a simple re-

---

[1] A first outline of this fully reversible (both abstract machine and implementation) architecture was presented in Thomsen, Glück, Axelsen, *Towards Designing a Reversible Processor Architecture*, *work-in-progress*, at the *1st Workshop on Reversible Computation, 2009* in York.

A. De Vos and R. Wille (Eds.): RC 2011, LNCS 7165, pp. 30–42, 2012.
© Springer-Verlag Berlin Heidelberg 2012

versible computing architecture for a reversible implementation of a Harvard architecture, Sect. 2. The architecture has a small instruction set but is still powerful enough to be Turing-complete in a reversible sense [3] and expressive enough to be the target for a compiler [1] from the high-level language Janus, Sect. 3.

The low-level implementation of Bob is designed with elementary reversible logic gates [5, 13] resulting in a robust technology-independent design, Sect. 4. It makes use of an extended version of the latest design of reversible arithmetic logic units [21], Sect. 4.1, and has a novel control structure that simplifies the address calculation compared to previous approaches [12,24], Sect. 4.2. As memory in reversible hardware is still an open question, we shall assume memory that is operationally reversible, such that the design is independent of any actual future memory implementation, regardless of whether this is based on conventional volatile memory [6] or reversible models like the *rotary element* [17]. For verification we implemented the design in Verilog. The programming was self-restricted to uphold the conventions of reversible logic design, Sect. 4.3.

2   The Problem of Control

In this section we describe the control logic used in our Harvard architecture, and the reasoning behind it.

In a conventional processor architecture, the address of the next instruction to be executed is often found by overwriting the program counter with a static address. As a result, the information about the old program counter is erased. If this is the case, then we do not know how to make a backwards step, *i.e.* irreversibility.

A solution to this problem could be to use the Landauer embedding [14] and generate a *trace* of all previous program counters. This approach, suggested by Cezzar [7], is not satisfactory. The trace, which would be as long as the number of executed instructions, is not part of the program's desired result and is an extremely wasteful use of memory. A processor which accumulates more and more garbage in this fashion is not practical.

Instead of using only a single register for program control (the program counter), we shall use an approach developed for the reversible von Neumann architecture Pendulum [12,24] as formalized in [4], where the address calculation of the reversible abstract machine relies on *three* special-purpose registers:

- *program counter* (pc): points at the current instruction in memory,
- *branch register* (br): contains information about the offset from the current to the next instruction, and
- *direction bit* (dir): specifies the current direction of execution; either FALSE (forward) or TRUE (backward).

The calculation of the next program counter (pc) now only depends on the branch register (br) and the direction bit (dir). If the value of the branch register is *zero*, then the execution will continue to the next instruction by adding 1

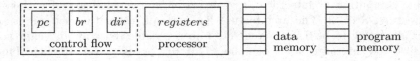

Fig. 1. The reversible Harvard architecture

to (or subtracting 1 from) the program counter, depending on the execution direction given by the direction bit. If the branch register contains a *non-zero* value then this is added to (or subtracted from) the program counter. In both cases the program counter is reversibly updated, and the branch register and direction bit are preserved. We therefore have enough information to do the *inverse* calculation to determine the previous instruction, *i.e.* reversibility.

Figure 1 shows the abstract reversible Harvard architecture. While a von Neumann architecture has only one memory containing both the program and data, they are separated in a Harvard architecture. This separation simplifies the reversible model by ensuring that a memory instruction cannot update its own instruction cell, which would lead to irreversibility.

3   A Simple Instruction Set Architecture, BobISA

The choice of the instruction set influences not only the expressiveness of the assembly language, but also the costs of the underlying hardware realization. A larger instruction set with many complex operations can increase the expressiveness and reduce code size, but will also result in higher costs in terms of gates, logic depth, ancillae, and so forth. We require that the reversible instruction set is *r-Turing complete* [3]; meaning that it can implement an interpreter for reversible Turing Machines without the use of a history, or other garbage [2]. Furthermore, all instructions are required to be *reversible updates* [4] and locally invertible. The rest of this section describes the 17 instructions of BobISA, divided into three types: arithmetic/logic instructions, branch instructions, and memory instructions.

3.1   Arithmetic-Logic Instructions

Table 1 shows the set of reversible arithmetic/logic instructions. It includes addition (ADD and ADD1), subtraction (SUB and SUB1), negation (NEG), and exclusive-or (XOR and XORI); the immediate instruction, XORI, computes exclusive-or with a given constant value. These are the basic instructions included in our reversible ALU design [21]. To ensure reversibility we use modular arithmetic.

Conventional processors typically allow multiplication and division by 2, implemented as left or right shifts. These are irreversible operations (*e.g.* the division by 2 deletes the least significant bit), so to circumvent this, left and right *roll* operations could be used instead. Here, we propose a novel solution with

Table 1. Arithmetic-logic instructions, their inverses and effect on registers R

i			$Inv(i)$	$Effect(i)$
ADD	reg_d	reg_s	SUB	$R(reg_d) \leftarrow R(reg_d) +_n R(reg_s)$
SUB	reg_d	reg_s	ADD	$R(reg_d) \leftarrow R(reg_d) -_n R(reg_s)$
ADD1	reg_d		SUB1	$R(reg_d) \leftarrow R(reg_d) +_n 1$
SUB1	reg_d		ADD1	$R(reg_d) \leftarrow R(reg_d) -_n 1$
NEG	reg_d		NEG	$R(reg_d) \leftarrow 0 -_n R(reg_d)$
XOR	reg_d	reg_s	XOR	$R(reg_d) \leftarrow R(reg_d) \oplus R(reg_s)$
XORI	reg_d	imm	XORI	$R(reg_d) \leftarrow R(reg_d) \oplus imm$
MUL2	reg_d		DIV2	$R(reg_d) \leftarrow mul2_n(R(reg_d))$
DIV2	reg_d		MUL2	$R(reg_d) \leftarrow div2_n(R(reg_d))$

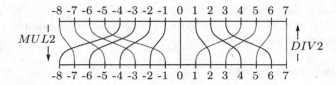

Fig. 2. Example of division (DIV2) and multiplication (MUL2) by 2 with 4-bit two's complement numbers. The solid blue lines show the inputs that are well defined.

a division/multiplication by 2 that conserves the sign of the two's complement numbers, but only returns the division or multiplication by 2 if the input is well-defined. For division, only the even numbers return the input value divided by 2, and multiplication only returns the input value multiplied by 2 if the input is small enough for it to double without overflow. The rest of the input values we map to values such that reversibility and local invertibility is assured and the instructions are easy to implement in logic. For a more intuitive description, Fig. 2 shows the mapping for 4-bit two's-complement numbers.

The multiplication/division operations are formally defined as

$$mul2_n(x) = \begin{cases} x \cdot 2 & \text{if } -2^{n-2} \leq x < 2^{n-2}, \\ x \cdot 2 - 2^n + 1 & \text{if } x \geq 2^{n-2}, \\ x \cdot 2 + 2^n + 1 & \text{if } x < -2^{n-2}, \end{cases} \quad (1)$$

and

$$div2_n(x) = \begin{cases} x/2 & \text{if } x \text{ is even,} \\ \frac{x-1}{2} + 2^{n-1} & \text{if } x \text{ is odd, and } x > 0, \\ \frac{x-1}{2} - 2^{n-1} & \text{if } x \text{ is odd, and } x < 0, \end{cases} \quad (2)$$

where n is the number of bits used in the representation of x.

A general restriction in reversible programming languages is that a register (or variable) must only be updated with a source value does not come from the register itself. (*E.g.* $a \leftarrow a - a$ is not allowed.) A violation of this will result in information destruction. The standard way of resolving this is by checking that the destination register reg_d and (second) source register reg_s are syntactically different. This check is simple at high abstraction levels, but implementing it at the logic level results in a large overhead. Also, if this check *fails* the whole program execution fails; it is hard at the logic circuit level to define the meaning of a failing architecture execution.

Instead, our solution is to slightly alter the memory model of the registers. When register reg_d is read, its value is swapped with 0. Now, if reg_s is the same as reg_d then the value of reg_s becomes 0 instead of the original value of reg_d, and so the value of register reg_d will not be destroyed. (*E.g.* $a := a - 0$ is calculated instead of $a := a - a$.) Writing values back to the register file is done in the opposite order: first the value of reg_s is swapped into the register reg_s, then afterwards the same for reg_d. In both writing cases the auxiliary value that is swapped in/out of the registers is 0.

3.2   Branch Instructions

Branch instructions are needed for control flow in programs. For BobISA, we have chosen four conditional branch, one unconditional branch, and two special swap-branch-register instructions for the instruction set (see Table 2).

The four conditional branch instructions were chosen for their simple implementation. Because we use two's complement numbers, both *greater-than-or-equal-to-zero* (BGEZ) and *less-than-zero* (BLZ) are simple checks of the most significant bit of the value in reg_d (FALSE for values greater than or equal to zero and TRUE if the value is less than zero). The other two conditional instructions are branches on *even* (BEVN) and *odd* (BODD) numbers. These are determined by a simple check of the *least* significant bit: a FALSE implies an even number and a TRUE implies an odd number. For all four instructions, if the branch condition evaluates to true then the offset (*off*) is *added* to the branch register; else, the branch register is left unchanged. There is also an unconditional branch instruction (BRA) that always updates the branch register with the given offset.

In conventional ISAs a *jump-and-link* instruction is used for procedure calls; it stores the current program counter in a register as a *return address* and then jumps to a given address. We know for Bob that the program counter is only updated by the branch register, so we can simulate the jump-and-link by loading an offset into the branch register, performing the jump and then have an instruction at the target address saving the branch register as a *return offset*.

There are two special instructions to support this: SWB and RSWB. The *swap-branch-register* (SWB) will swap the value of a given register with the value of the branch register. The *swap-branch-register-and-reverse* (RSWB) will do the same, and furthermore reverse the execution direction by flipping the direction bit.

This can be used for inverse procedure calls. The use of the RSWB instruction is novel and was chosen because it simplifies the logic for the pc update significantly, reducing the gate count and logic depth compared to previous designs [12,24,4].

3.3   Memory Instruction

The usual *load/store* memory instructions in conventional instruction sets are, by themselves, irreversible. However, by combining the load and the store instructions into a single *exchange* (EXCH) instruction, the result is a memory instruction that is reversible and self-inverse (as shown in Table 2), cf. [12,24]. This takes a register (reg_d) that contains some value to be exchanged into memory and a register (reg_a) that contains the address of the cell in memory that we want to exchange, as arguments. The value in the register and the value at the address in the memory are then swapped.

Table 2. Branch and memory instructions, their inverses, and effect on the general purpose registers R, special purpose registers br and dir, and data memory M

i		$Inv(i)$		$Effect(i)$
BGEZ reg_d off		BGEZ reg_d $-off$		$br \leftarrow br +_n (R(reg_d) \geq 0$? off : $0)$
BLZ reg_d off		BLZ reg_d $-off$		$br \leftarrow br +_n (R(reg_d) < 0$? off : $0)$
BEVN reg_d off		BEVN reg_d $-off$		$br \leftarrow br +_n (even(R(reg_d))$? off : $0)$
BODD reg_d off		BODD reg_d $-off$		$br \leftarrow br +_n (odd(R(reg_d))$? off : $0)$
BRA off		BRA $-off$		$br \leftarrow br +_n off$
SWB reg_d		SWB reg_d		$br \leftrightarrow R(reg_d)$
RSWB reg_d		RSWB reg_d		$br \leftrightarrow R(reg_d)$; $dir \leftarrow \neg dir$
EXCH reg_d reg_a		EXCH reg_d reg_a		$R(reg_d) \leftrightarrow M(R(reg_a))$

4   The Architecture of the Reversible Machine, Bob

Based on the ISA above we design an architecture, called *Bob*, that performs one instruction within a single clock-cycle. We have chosen a 16-bit architecture, which leads to the following design properties and the defined instruction encoding shown in Fig. 3.

- *Registers* - 4 bits for register numbering allows for 16 registers in total, each with a size of 16 bits. Using two's complement representation, numbers can range from -32768 through 32767.
- *Memory* - We can index 2^{16} words of 16 bits (the maximum size we can load into the registers). This gives a memory cap of 128 KB.
- *Jumps* - With an offset length of 8 bits, a branch-jump can not be of more than 127 lines. However, jumps can be arbitrarily long by the using the SWB instruction.
- *Immediates* - With 8 bits, immediate values must range from -128 to 127.

bits:	15			12	11			8	7			4	3			0
Arith & mem		*opcode*				reg_d				reg_s				*arith*		
Branch & imm		*opcode*				reg_d						*off/imm*				
ADD	1	1	0	0		reg_d				reg_s			0	1	0	0
SUB	1	1	0	0		reg_d				reg_s			1	1	0	1
ADD1	1	1	0	0		reg_d			0	0	0	0	0	1	1	0
SUB1	1	1	0	0		reg_d			0	0	0	0	1	1	1	1
NEG	1	1	0	0		reg_d			0	0	0	0	0	1	1	1
XOR	1	1	0	0		reg_d				reg_s			0	0	0	0
XORI	0	0	0	0		reg_d						*imm*				
MUL2	1	0	1	0		reg_d			0	0	0	0	0	0	0	0
DIV2	1	0	0	1		reg_d			0	0	0	0	0	0	0	0
EXCH	1	0	0	0		reg_d				reg_a			0	0	0	0
BGEZ	0	0	1	1		reg_d						*off*				
BLZ	0	0	1	0		reg_d						*off*				
BEVN	0	1	0	1		reg_d						*off*				
BODD	0	1	0	0		reg_d						*off*				
BRA	0	0	0	1	0	0	0	0				*off*				
RSWB	0	1	1	1		reg_d			0	0	0	0	0	0	0	0
SWB	0	1	1	0		reg_d			0	0	0	0	0	0	0	0

Fig. 3. Instruction formats and instruction set encoding for Bob

- *Register zero* - Register 0, reg_0 is assumes to always contain the value 0. Instructions with only one register (NEG, ADD1, etc.) are implemented with this requirement in mind (*e.g.* ADD1 reg_d is implemented as $R(reg_d) \leftarrow R(reg_d) +_n R(reg_0) +_n 1$).[2]

While it is a primary requirement for us to keep the implementation *garbage-free*, we also try to reduce the number of ancillae bits, and keep circuit size at a minimum. We therefore accept that the delay of sub-circuits (*e.g.*, the ALU and adders) are linear with respect to the number of input bits, as this lowers the above costs.

Figure 4 shows a detailed design of the processor, and Table 3 shows the gate count. Even though it has many similarities with the MIPS R2000 processor [18], there are some significant differences. Notice, for example, that preserving information everywhere implies that the control signals from the control logic unit can not be deleted, but have to be uncomputed using an *inverse control logic unit*. Other significantly different parts are the *arithmetic logic unit* and the *address calculation logic*, which will be described below.

---

[2] Breaking the assumption about register 0 will *not* break reversibility of the architecture, but only result it a processor that do not behave as expected; *e.g.* the example with ADD1.

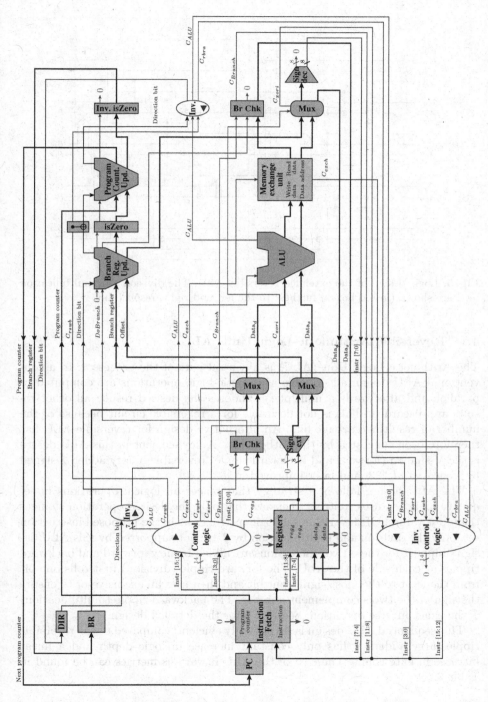

Fig. 4. The logic design of the reversible processor. The black dots indicate split and merge of lines, *not* fan-out and fan-in. The small blue arrows indicates input and output control lines. The light blue boxes are memory elements, the brown polygons are the ALU and other adders, and the small green figures are minor combinational circuits.

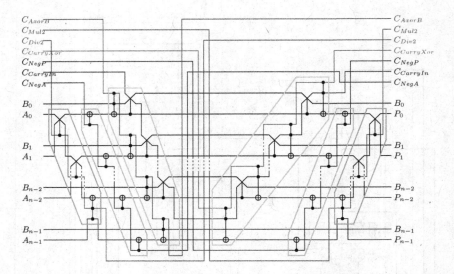

Fig. 5. Logic design of the extended reversible ALU. The division and multiplication by 2 are shown (in red boxes) furthest to the left and right, respectably.

4.1   Reversible Arithmetic-Logic Unit, ALU

The Arithmetic Logic Unit (ALU) is a central part of the processor. In a conventional ALU design all possible arithmetic-logic operations are computed in parallel, and afterwards a multiplexer chooses the desired result; all other results are discarded. This is not desirable for a reversible circuit because of the number of resulting garbage bits. An alternative design for reversible ALU has therefore been suggested by the authors [21]. A key element in this ALU design is the V-shaped (forward and backward ripple) reversible binary adder designed by Vedral et al. [23] and later improved in [8, 22, 20].

The ALU design follows a strategy that places all logical operations in sequence and then uses controls to ensure that only the desired operation changes the input values. Of the arithmetic-logic instructions in the proposed instruction set, only the division and multiplication by 2 are not supported by this ALU design. Support for these two instructions are added by new forward and backward ripples at each side of the ALU. The forward ripple (division) first rolls one bit from the least to the most significant bit and then uses an exclusive-or to ensure the sign of the two's complement number. The backward ripple (multiplication) is the exact inverse operation. See Fig. 5 for the detailed design.

This sequential ALU design is surprisingly efficient: compared to the reversible ripple-carry adders it has only constant increase in logic depth and a linear increase in gate count. The cost of the ALU in various metrics can be found in Table 3.

Table 3. Costs in various metrics of the extended n-bit ALU compared to an optimized reversible ripple-carry adder and the entire Bob design without memory.

	Reversible n-bit adder [22]	Extended n-bit ALU	Bob architecture without memory
Gate count total	$4n - 2$	$8n - 4$	473
Feynman gates	$2n$	$2n$	155
Toffoli gates	0	$2n + 2$	146
Fredkin gates	$2n - 2$	$4n - 6$	172
Ancillae bits	1	0	39
Logic depth	$3n - 1$	$3n + 3$	
Logic width	$2n + 1$	$2n + 7$	

4.2 Address Calculation

The address calculation depends both on the semantics of the overall architecture and the instruction set: the architecture specifies in which order to update the special purpose registers (pc, br, dir), while the choice of branch instructions determines the register updates. Adapting the previously described semantics for reversible control (Sect. 2), the address calculation in Bob has the following steps, cf. Fig. 4.

1. *Branch check.* We check if the current instruction is a branch instruction; in the case of a conditional branch instruction we also check if the condition is satisfied. If both evaluate to true, a *doBranch* signal to update the branch register is sent.
2. *Swapping branch register.* Now, we decide what to update. Often, it will be the value in the branch register, but if the current instruction is a swap-branch-register instruction (SWB or RSWB), then we must update the value of the given general purpose register instead. To do this we use a 2:2 reversible multiplexer (implemented using an array of Fredkin gates), where a control line decides if the inputs are swapped.
3. *Updating the branch register.* If *doBranch* is TRUE then the value of the branch register is updated with the value of the offset. The offset is added if the direction bit is FALSE (forward execution), otherwise subtracted if the direction bit is TRUE (backwards execution), using a simplified ALU.
4. *Updating the direction bit.* In case of an RSWB instruction we must invert the direction bit; this is done with a controlled-not gate.
5. *Updating the program counter.* If the updated branch offset equals 0, then the program counter is updated with 1 to step one instruction ahead. Otherwise the program counter is updated with the value of the branch register. Again, the update is either addition or subtraction depending on the direction bit and implemented with a simplified ALU.

```
module alu
  (input  [15:0] A, B
  ,input  C_negA,  C_carryIn,   C_AxorB,   C_carryXor,   C_negP,   C_div2,   C_mul2
  ,output [15:0] P, B_o
  ,output C_negA_o, C_carryIn_o, C_AxorB_o, C_carryXor_o, C_negP_o, C_div2_o, C_mul2_o
  );
    wire [15:0] tmp1, tmp2, tmp3, tmp4, tmp5;
  // DIV2
    assign tmp1[13:0] = (C_div2 ? A[14:1] : A[13:0]);
    assign tmp1[15]   = A[15];
    assign tmp1[14]   = (C_div2 ? A[15] ^ A[0] : A[14]);
  // ADD, SUB, NEG, XOR
    assign tmp2 = (C_negA ? ~tmp1    : tmp1);
    assign tmp3 = (C_carryIn ? tmp2 + 1 : tmp2);
    assign tmp4 = (C_carryXor ? tmp3 + B : (C_AxorB ? tmp3 ^ B : tmp3));
    assign tmp5 = (C_negP ? ~tmp4    : tmp4);
  // MUL2
    assign P[14:1] = (C_mul2 ? tmp5[13:0] : tmp5[14:1]);
    assign P[15]   = tmp5[15];
    assign P[0]    = (C_mul2 ? tmp5[15] ^ tmp5[14] : tmp5[0]);
endmodule
```

Fig. 6. Verilog module for the ALU. Assignments to unchanged outwires (denoted by "*wirename_*o") have been removed for brevity.

6. *Inverse branch check.* To perform the address calculation more efficiently some temporary control values are used, and the final step is to uncompute these. For this, we use the exact inverse of the branch check, explained in the first step.

Previous designs [12,24], which use an *unconditional-branch-and-reverse* instruction to reverse the execution direction, cf. [4], requires two adders in the update of the branch register, compared to one adder for our design.

4.3 Verification

To test the correctness of the design, a Verilog program was implemented and simulated using ModelSim. This language and tool has no built-in support for reversible circuits, but by imposing the Verilog program with the restriction of only using reversible updates, this simulation verifies the correctness of the design. As an example, Fig. 6 shows the implementation of the ALU module. The entire Bob implementation is about 800 lines of pretty-printed code and uses 20 modules. We will not report on timing and other results from this simulation, as these do not yield any additional insights into the design of the architecture.

A future implementation using a *reversible* specification language, such as SyReC [26], is desirable. The effect on the cost of such an implementation compared to custom design of Bob (see Table 3) is hard to predict and depends on the abstraction level of the implementation.

5   Conclusion

We have presented the design of a purely reversible computing architecture with a novel and efficient address calculation and a small, but expressive instruction set containing 17 locally-invertible instructions.[3] The instruction set is r-Turing complete and well-suited as the target language of a compiler from existing high-level structured reversible programming languages. The logical design uses in total only 473 reversible gates (see Table 3), which amounts to 6328 transistors in the *adiabatic dual-line pass-transister* technology [9].

This demonstrates that the design of a complete reversible computing architecture, as presented in this paper, can serve as the core of a simple programmable reversible computing system. Even though our reversible computing architecture does not offer the advanced and sophisticated features of mainstream general-purpose computers, the simplicity makes our design suited as part of special-purpose embedded systems that works without user interaction.

Clearly, further work is required both on the hardware side (including the design and synthesis of reversible circuits with different technologies), as well as on the software side, for fully reaping the low-power benefits of reversible computing systems. This is especially true for the implementation or interfacing of memory.

References

1. Axelsen, H.B.: Clean Translation of an Imperative Reversible Programming Language. In: Knoop, J. (ed.) CC 2011. LNCS, vol. 6601, pp. 144–163. Springer, Heidelberg (2011)
2. Axelsen, H.B., Glück, R.: A Simple and Efficient Universal Reversible Turing Machine. In: Dediu, A.-H., Inenaga, S., Martín-Vide, C. (eds.) LATA 2011. LNCS, vol. 6638, pp. 117–128. Springer, Heidelberg (2011)
3. Axelsen, H.B., Glück, R.: What Do Reversible Programs Compute? In: Hofmann, M. (ed.) FOSSACS 2011. LNCS, vol. 6604, pp. 42–56. Springer, Heidelberg (2011)
4. Axelsen, H.B., Glück, R., Yokoyama, T.: Reversible Machine Code and Its Abstract Processor Architecture. In: Diekert, V., Volkov, M.V., Voronkov, A. (eds.) CSR 2007. LNCS, vol. 4649, pp. 56–69. Springer, Heidelberg (2007)
5. Barenco, A., Bennett, C.H., Cleve, R., DiVincenzo, D.P., Margolus, N., Shor, P., Sleator, T., Smolin, J.A., Weinfurter, H.: Elementary gates for quantum computation. Physical Review A 52(5), 3457–3467 (1995)
6. Burignat, S., Thomsen, M.K., Klimczak, M., Olczak, M., De Vos, A.: Interfacing Reversible Pass-Transistor CMOS Chips with Conventional Restoring CMOS Circuits. In: De Vos, A., Wille, R. (eds.) RC 2011. LNCS, vol. 7156, pp. 113–123. Springer, Heidelberg (2012)
7. Cezzar, R.: The design of a processor architecture capable of forward and reverse execution. In: IEEE Proceedings of the SOUTHEASTCON 1991, vol. 2, pp. 885–890. IEEE (1991)

---

[3] As a historical remark, EDSAC in 1949 had about the same number of irreversible instructions.

8. Cuccaro, S.A., Draper, T.G., Kutin, S.A., Moulton, D.P.: A new quantum ripple-carry addition circuit. arXiv:quant-ph/0410184v1 (2005)
9. De Vos, A.: Reversible Computing: Fundamentals, Quantum Computing and Applications. Wiley-VCH (2010)
10. De Vos, A., Burignat, S., Thomsen, M.K.: Reversible implementation of a discrete integer linear transformation. Journal of Multiple-Valued Logic and Soft Computing 18(1), 25–35 (2012)
11. Feynman, R.P.: Feynman Lectures on Computation. Addison-Wesley (1996)
12. Frank, M.P.: Reversibility for Efficient Computing. Ph.D. thesis, EECS Department, Massachusetts Institute of Technology (1999)
13. Fredkin, E., Toffoli, T.: Conservative logic. International Journal of Theoretical Physics 21(3-4), 219–253 (1982)
14. Landauer, R.: Irreversibility and heat generation in the computing process. IBM Journal of Research and Development 5(3), 183–191 (1961)
15. Lutz, C.: Janus: A time-reversible language. A letter to R. Landauer (1986), http://www.tetsuo.jp/ref/janus.html
16. Maslov, D., Dueck, G., Miller, D.: Synthesis of Fredkin-Toffoli reversible networks. IEEE Transactions on Very Large Scale Integration (VLSI) Systems 13(6), 765–769 (2005)
17. Morita, K.: A Simple Universal Logic Element and Cellular Automata for Reversible Computing. In: Margenstern, M., Rogozhin, Y. (eds.) MCU 2001. LNCS, vol. 2055, pp. 102–113. Springer, Heidelberg (2001)
18. Patterson, D.A., Hennessy, J.L.: Computer Organization & Design: the hardware/software interface, 2nd edn. Morgan Kaufmann Publishers (1997)
19. Shende, V., Bullock, S., Markov, I.: Synthesis of quantum-logic circuits. IEEE Transactions on Computer-Aided Design of Integrated Circuits and Systems 25(6), 1000–1010 (2006)
20. Thomsen, M.K., Axelsen, H.B.: Parallelization of reversible ripple-carry adders. Parallel Processing Letters 19(1), 205–222 (2009)
21. Thomsen, M.K., Glück, R., Axelsen, H.B.: Reversible arithmetic logic unit for quantum arithmetic. Journal of Physics A: Mathematical and Theoretical 43(38), 382002 (2010)
22. Van Rentergem, Y., De Vos, A.: Optimal design of a reversible full adder. International Journal of Unconventional Computing 1(4), 339–355 (2005)
23. Vedral, V., Barenco, A., Ekert, A.: Quantum networks for elementary arithmetic operations. Physical Review A 54(1), 147–153 (1996)
24. Vieri, C.J.: Reversible Computer Engineering and Architecture. Ph.D. thesis, EECS Department, Massachusetts Institute of Technology (1999)
25. Wille, R., Drechsler, R.: Towards a Design Flow for Reversible Logic. Springer Science (2010)
26. Wille, R., Offermann, S., Drechsler, R.: SyReC: A programming language for synthesis of reversible circuits. In: Proceedings of the Forum on Specification & Design Languages, pp. 1–6. IET, Southhampton (2010)
27. Yokoyama, T., Axelsen, H.B., Glück, R.: Principles of a reversible programming language. In: Proceedings of Computing Frontiers, pp. 43–54. ACM (2008)
28. Yokoyama, T., Glück, R.: A reversible programming language and its invertible self-interpreter. In: Proceedings of Partial Evaluation and Program Manipulation, pp. 144–153. ACM (2007)

Optimization of Reversible Circuits Using Reconfigured Templates

Md. Mazder Rahman[1], Gerhard W. Dueck[1], and Anindita Banerjee[2]

[1] Faculty of Computer Science, University of New Brunswick, Canada
[2] Department of Physics and Material Science Engineering, JIIT, Noida, India

Abstract. This paper presents a new method to optimize the quantum costs of reversible circuits. A single quantum implementation of the Toffoli-3 gate has been used to decompose reversible circuits into quantum circuits. Reconfigured quantum templates using splitting rules are introduced. The Controlled-NOT, Controlled-V, and Controlled-V^+ gates can be split into two gates – splitting rules are derived from this fact. Quantum costs of reversible circuits are measured by the number of two-qubit operations. Therefore, the costs of reconfigured templates will be unchanged when the splitting rules are applied. Although the number of quantum gates of reconfigured templates increases, their quantum cost remains invariant. Experimental results show that significant cost reductions can be achieved with the proposed method.

Keywords: Logic Synthesis, Reversible Logic, Quantum Circuit, Entangled State, Quantum Cost, Quantum Templates.

1 Introduction

Synthesis of reversible logic has gained significant attention due to its potential application in low power design [1]. Infinite state space of information at the quantum level can be achieved by transforming information through quantum gates as well as quantum circuits [2]. Operations in quantum circuits are inherently reversible and the resemblance of a qubit in quantum computing to a bit in classical logic is obvious [3], as a result, researchers are interested in synthesis of reversible circuits and their quantum implementation. The synthesis of reversible logic circuits using elementary quantum gates is different from classical logic synthesis (irreversible) methods. Therefore, different synthesis methods have been proposed to obtain cascades of reversible gates. These methods include: transformation based algorithms [4], [5], translating ESOP expression into Toffoli circuits [6] and others. At the quantum level, reversible gates are decomposed into elementary quantum gates [7]. After the decomposition, the quantum level circuits can still be optimized [8].

Optimization approaches, such as template matching [9], [8] focus on the reduction of the gate count or quantum cost (number of quantum primitives) of a Toffoli network by finding gate sequences in circuits that can be replaced with sequences of lower cost. It has been shown that two 2-qubit elementary

A. De Vos and R. Wille (Eds.): RC 2011, LNCS 7165, pp. 43–53, 2012.
© Springer-Verlag Berlin Heidelberg 2012

quantum gates that act on the same two qubit lines can be merged into a new quantum gate of cost one [10], also referred to as a double gate of unit cost [11]. A finite set of two-qubit quantum gates has been proposed in [12]. Since a sequence of quantum primitives acting on the same two qubits can be treated as a single operation of cost one, quantum circuits can be synthesized considering this metric. A quantum circuit with minimum number of gates is preferable, if both circuits have the same number of two-qubit operations. However, if an identity has two different quantum implementations with the same number of two-qubit operations then both of these identity circuits can be used as quantum templates to reduce the number of gates in quantum circuits.

It was observed, that reconfigured quantum templates using splitting rules play a significant role in optimizing quantum costs of quantum circuits as explained in detail in subsequent sections. Before the optimization process, reversible circuits comprised of Multiple Control Toffoli (MCT) gates are decomposed into quantum circuits by the substitution of a unique quantum implementation of Toffoli-3, and then apply reconfigured templates in the optimization phase. Finally, the number of two-qubit gates in circuits are found using moving rules to calculate the quantum costs of the circuits.

The remainder of this paper is structured as follows. Section 2 presents the necessary background of reversible logic theory, quantum operations as well as two-qubit operations of unit cost. Section 3 reviews the published quantum templates and introduces reconfigured templates. Section 4 shows the details of the new template matching algorithm. Experimental results for benchmark functions are shown in Section 5. Section 6 concludes the paper.

2   Background

A reversible function is defined as one to one mapping, i.e. each element in the input vector uniquely maps to an element in the output vector. Reversible functions can be realized by cascades of reversible gates without feedback and fan-out. Reversible gates, such as Toffoli [13], Peres [14] and Fredkin [15], are conventionally used to synthesize reversible circuits. Reversible circuits realized by the generalized Toffoli-n gate (where $1 \leq n$) are referred to as MCT circuits.

In contrast to the logic representations in classical reversible circuits, the logic representations in quantum cirucits are quite different. The fundamental information in quantum computing is a qubit – analogous to a bit in classical logic. An arbitrary qubit is defined by the state vector $|\psi\rangle = \alpha|0\rangle + \beta|1\rangle$ where α and β are complex numbers that satisfy: $|\alpha|^2 + |\beta|^2 = 1$. Similarly a generalized two qubit state can be described as

$$|\psi\rangle = \lambda_1|00\rangle + \lambda_2|01\rangle + \lambda_3|10\rangle + \lambda_4|11\rangle = \begin{pmatrix} \lambda_1 \\ \lambda_2 \\ \lambda_3 \\ \lambda_4 \end{pmatrix}.$$

This state is separable as tensor product of two states if and only if $\lambda_1\lambda_4 = \lambda_2\lambda_3$ otherwise the state is said to be entangled. This condition can be easily visualized if the tensor product of two single qubit states are considered; denoted by $\alpha|0\rangle + \beta|1\rangle$ and $\alpha'|0\rangle + \beta'|1\rangle$. The resulting two-qubit state can be represented as

$$\begin{pmatrix} \alpha \\ \beta \end{pmatrix} \otimes \begin{pmatrix} \alpha' \\ \beta' \end{pmatrix} = \begin{pmatrix} \alpha\alpha' \\ \alpha\beta' \\ \beta\alpha' \\ \beta\beta' \end{pmatrix}$$

that satisfies the condition of separability as $\alpha\alpha'\beta\beta' = \alpha\beta'\beta\alpha'$.

Moreover, the elementary quantum gates NOT, Controlled-NOT, Controlled-V and Controlled-V^+ are represented by unitary matrices [10] that may include complex elements. For example, the unitary matrix of the two-qubit Controlled-V gate is

$$M_v = \begin{bmatrix} 1 & 0 & 0 & 0 \\ 0 & 1 & 0 & 0 \\ 0 & 0 & \frac{(1+i)}{2} & \frac{(1-i)}{2} \\ 0 & 0 & \frac{(1-i)}{2} & \frac{(1+i)}{2} \end{bmatrix}$$

M_v will not produce entangled states for binary-valued inputs. Two-qubit quantum primitives Controlled-V and Controlled-V^+ are the Controlled-$sqrt$-of-NOT, where Controlled-NOT is self-inverse and Controlled-V and Controlled-V^+ are inverses of each other. Therefore, any one primitive among these three can be formed by cascading the other two primitives, referred to as splitting rules that are shown in Fig. 1. Two more splitting rules are obtained by interchanging Controlled-V and Controlled-V^+ in Fig. 1. In quantum computation, the splitting of a quantum primitive does not increase the number of two-qubit operations.

The quantum cost of a circuit is usually defined as the number of quantum primitives required to realize the circuit. However, here a modified metric is used. Recall that any two-qubit quantum gate is realizable by an operation of unit cost [12]. In this paper the quantum costs of circuits is the number of two-qubit operations rather than the number of quantum primitives. It is clear that the number of two-qubit operations will never be greater than the number of quantum primitives. According to Lemma 6.1 in [7], the classical reversible Toffoli-3 gate has a quantum implementation of five quantum primitives as shown in Fig. 2(b). Note that, the right most Controlled-V gate can move anywhere in the circuit; control lines x_2 and x_3 can be swapped; as well as Controlled-V and Controlled-V^+ can be replaced with each other in the circuit. Therefore, different arrangements of quantum implementations of Toffoli-3 are possible. However, any one of these

Fig. 1. Splitting of two-qubit quantum primitives

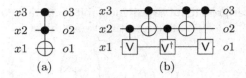

Fig. 2. Reversible circuits: (a) Toffoli-3, (b) quantum implementation

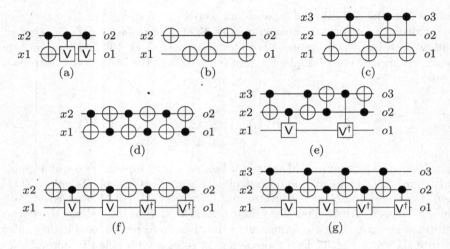

Fig. 3. Quantum templates

quantum implementations can be used when decomposing reversible circuits. The quantum costs of reversible Toffoli-3 is five.

3   Quantum Templates

If two quantum circuits C_1 and C_2 that realize the functions f and f^{-1} respectively, then C_1C_2 realize the identity function. The fundamental concepts of templates come from the quantum realization of the identity function. A quantum template is a circuit of quantum primitives that realizes the identity function. The quantum templates published in [8] are shown in Fig. 3.

The general idea of template matching is that, if a sequence of more than half of the quantum primitives in a template match a sequence of gates in the circuit to be optimized, then this sequence can be replaced with the inverse of remaining primitives in the template. The interested reader can find more details about quantum templates and simplification of quantum circuits in [8]. Here the template matching algorithm with the incorporation of splitting rules as well as new cost metrics is to be discussed. In [8], the quantum costs is measured by the number of quantum primitives required to realize the circuit. However, in this paper the number of two-qubit operations are used, rather than counting quantum primitives. Since a template is an identity circuit, a quantum gate at any either end of a circuit can move to other end, resulting in an identity function as well. The quantum costs of all two-qubit templates in Fig. 3(a), (b), (d) and (e) have costs of 1. However, the quantum costs of the template shown in Fig. 3(e) is 4 rather than 6 since the last Controlled-*NOT* gate can move to the first position resulting in 4 two-qubit operations. According to our new cost metric, quantum costs of templates in Fig. 3(c) and (g) are 5 and 8 respectively. Note that, the reverse of an identity circuit is also an identity circuit. Therefore, the reverse of a template is also a template.

Observation 1. *The quantum templates in Fig. 3(c), (e) and (g) can be derived from two Toffoli-3 gates that realize an identity circuit as shown in Fig. 4(a).*

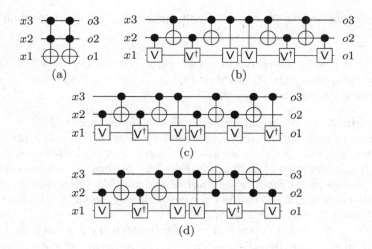

Fig. 4. Identity circuits derived from two Toffoli-3 gates

Since the Toffoli-3 has different quantum implementations of cost five, the identity circuit in Fig. 4(a) can be decomposed in three different ways: by flipping and inverting the quantum implementation of first Toffoli-3 for 2nd Toffoli-3 and swapping the control lines of 2nd Toffoli-3 in its quantum decomposition as shown in Fig. 4(b), (c) and (d) respectively.

For the first case, two Controlled-V gates 4 and 5 (gates are numbered from left to right starting at 0) in the circuit in Fig. 4(b) can be merged into a Controlled-NOT gate, gates 3 and 6 can be deleted, gates 0 and 9 can be merged into a Controlled-NOT, and finally two Controlled-V^{+} gates 2 and 7 can be merged into a Controlled-NOT gate. The resulting circuit is exactly the same sequence of quantum gates as in the template in Fig. (c). For the second case, the gates 4 and 9 in the circuit shown in Fig. 4(c) can be moved together and deleted and the obtained circuit is the same as the quantum template in Fig. 3(g). Finally, gates 4 and 5 in the circuit shown in Fig. 4(d) can be merged into one, similarly

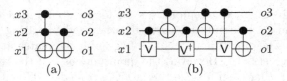

Fig. 5. Reversible circuits: (a) MCT realization, (b) Quantum decomposition

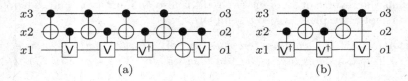

Fig. 6. Quantum circuits: (a) Reconfigured template, (b) Optimized quantum circuit

gates 0 and 9 can be moved together and merged into a Controlled-NOT gate. After that by applying the template in Fig. 3(c), the resulting circuit is exactly the same as the template in Fig. 3(e).

Observation 2. *Consider the reversible circuit shown in Fig. 5(a).*

According to different quantum implementations of Toffoli-3 of costs 5, there are different quantum decompositions of circuit in Fig. 5(a). However, by using quantum implementation of Toffoli-3 in Fig. 2(b), the quantum decomposition of the circuit as shown in Fig. 5(b) can not be optimized by the template matching method. Whereas the other quantum decomposition of circuit in Fig. 5(a) can be optimized using templates in Fig. 3.

However, if the last Controlled-V of the template in Fig. 3(g) is split, as shown in Fig. 6(a), this reconfigured template can be applied to the circuit shown in Fig. 5(b), and the optimized circuit also has cost 5 as shown in Fig. 6(b).

Observation 3. *If the number of two-qubit operations in quantum circuits is considered as the cost metric, then the splitting rule does not increase the cost of the template. It can also be noticed that the template of costs 5 as shown in Fig. 3(c) can be reconfigured by using splitting rules as the circuit of costs 5 shown in Fig. 7(a). By using the moving rule, the gates sequence can be rearranged as shown in Fig. 7(b) and the last 4 gates can be replaced by the first 3 gates reducing the gate count in quantum circuits. Therefore, one of the following two reconfigured templates along with the template in Fig. 3(c) can be used to optimize quantum circuits.*

From observation 3 it can inferred that splitting rules can be used in either templates or in circuits. In our work splitting rules are used in templates to generate reconfigured templates. However, different arrangements of gates sequence in templates are possible by using splitting and moving rules. This is illustrated in the applications of reconfigured templates in the subsequent sections.

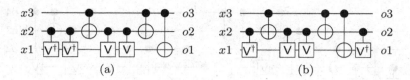

Fig. 7. Quantum templates: (a) Splitting gate, (b) Reconfigured templates

4   Template Matching Algorithm

In template matching, the first gate of a template can be matched with an equivalent gate anywhere in the circuit and the subsequent gates of template can be matched either in forward direction or in backward direction [8],[9]. In our implementation of template matching algorithm, we considered only the forward direction procedure for searching the gates sequence to be optimized into a circuit. A set of reconfigured templates alone with published templates has been applied in template matching.

Example 1. Consider the function realized by the Toffoli-4 gate. Its decomposition (using Toffoli-3 gates) with one extra working line, w, is shown in Fig. 8. The resulting quantum circuit with 20 quantum primitives can be obtained by substituting the quantum implementation of Toffoli-3 gates shown in Fig. 9.

If the templates from [8] are applied to the circuit in Fig. 9, then a circuit with 15 quantum primitives is obtained as shown in Fig. 10. However, different substitutions of Toffoli-3 may lead to sub-optimal circuits. But it is not feasible to keep track of what specific substitution of quantum implementation of Toffoli-3 leads to the circuit with the lowest cost. Reconfigured templates offer an alternative solution. A unique quantum implementation of Toffoli-3 can be used to decompose reversible circuits into quantum circuits. The reconfigured template shown in Fig. 7(b) can be applied to circuit in Fig. 10 and this results in the well known quantum circuit of costs 14 which is also the number of two-qubit operations into the circuit. The quantum implementation of higher ordered Toffoli gates with exactly the same number of quantum primitives reported in [8] were also obtained. In all cases a single quantum implementation of Toffoli-3 has been used in the substitution and reconfigured templates were applied.

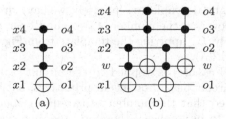

Fig. 8. Reversible circuits: (a) Toffoli-4, (b) MCT realization

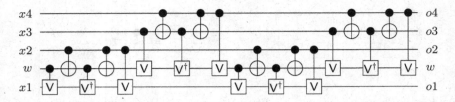

Fig. 9. Quantum decomposition of Toffoli-4

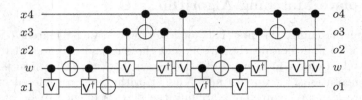

Fig. 10. After applying the templates in Fig. 3

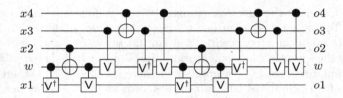

Fig. 11. Best reported quantum realization of Toffoli-4 of costs 14

Example 2. Consider the function 3_17_13 (taken from RevLib [16]). Its MCT realization and quantum decomposition are shown in Fig. 12(a) and (b) respectively.

Applying the templates in Fig. 3 to the circuit in Fig. 12(b), results in circuit shown in Fig. 12(c) with 12 quantum primitives. The number of two-qubit operations in the circuit is 8. However, reconfigured templates can be applied for further optimization. Now, it can be seen that either one of the two reconfigured templates in Fig. 3(e) and (g) can be applied to the circuit in Fig. 12(c). After applying these reconfigured templates separately, we have circuits of 11 quantum gates in both cases. However, the number of two-qubit operations in the circuits are 7 and 8 respectively. By applying the template from Fig. 3(g) we obtain the circuit shown in Fig. 12(d).

If the template in Fig. 3(e) is applied to the circuit in Fig. 12(d) then the resulting optimized circuit has 10 quantum primitives, as shown in Fig. 12(e). It should also be noted that the number of two-qubit operations in circuit is 7 (moving rules need to be applied), therefore, the quantum cost of reversible benchmark 3_17_13 is 7 which is the lowest reported cost.

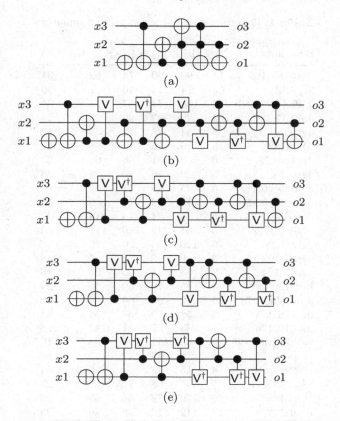

Fig. 12. (a) Benchmark MCT circuit 3_17_13, (b) its quantum decomposition, (c) after applying the templates from Fig. 3(e), (d) circuit obtained from 12(c) by applying the reconfigured template from Fig. 3(g), (e) optimized circuit with quantum costs 7

5   Experimental Results

The template matching algorithm was implemented using RevKit-1.0 [17] tools. The program was run for several reversible benchmark MCT circuits provided in RevLib [16]. A small selection of the results are shown in Table 1. The third column represents the costs of benchmarks reported in RevLib. After decomposing higher order Toffoli gates, Toffoli-3 gates were substituted by a unique quantum implementation of costs five. Before running template matching, 22 reconfigured templates were generated and these were applied together with the previously reported templates. The fifth column shows the total number of two-qubit gates in circuits represents the quantum costs of quantum circuits which is also considered as the quantum costs of original reversible circuits. Moreover, our implementation reduces the costs of reversible circuits by approximate 30% on average and in some cases cost reductions of over 50% have been achieved.

Table 1. Quantum cost reduction using templates

Benchmarks	N_L	$C[16]$	N_{QG}^D	N_{QG}^T	QC_{2q}	$C_{RD}(\%)$
0410184_169	14	90	90	74	62	31
3_17_13	3	14	14	10	7	50
4_49_16	5	60	74	57	51	31
4_49_17	4	32	32	26	23	28
4gt10-v1_81	5	34	48	42	40	17
4gt11_82	5	16	16	14	8	50
4gt4-v0_78	6	53	81	68	64	21
4gt5_76	5	29	36	30	26	28
4mod5-v0_18	5	25	25	11	9	64
4mod5-v0_19	5	13	13	10	9	31
4mod5-v1_23	5	24	24	14	14	42
alu-v2_31	5	101	143	116	111	22
cnt3-5_180	16	120	155	126	126	18
ham3_102	3	9	9	7	5	44
ham7_104	7	83	111	95	91	18
hwb4_49	5	65	79	60	56	29
mini-alu_167	5	62	90	66	64	29
mod10_171	5	58	79	57	54	32
mod10_176	5	43	57	41	41	28
mod5adder_128	6	83	111	99	93	16
mod5d2_70	5	16	16	12	10	38
rd32-v1_68	4	13	13	7	6	54
rd53_135	7	77	98	75	75	23
rd73_140	10	76	76	55	55	28
rd84_142	15	112	112	86	86	23

- N_L: Number of lines with extra working lines for decomposition
- $C[16]$: Reported costs in RevLib pages [16].
- N_{QG}^D: Number of quantum gates after Toffoli decomposition of Benchmarks
- N_{QG}^T: Number of quantum gates after template matching
- QC_{2q}: Quantum costs as the number of 2-qubit quantum gates
- $C_{RD}(\%)$: Costs reductions in percentage from decomposition to template matching.

6   Conclusion

In this paper, we have shown the effectiveness of reconfigured templates in reducing the quantum costs of reversible circuits where a unique quantum implementation of the Toffoli-3 gate has been used in decomposition of larger Toffoli gates. We observed that different quantum implementation of Toffoli-3 results different quantum costs when only templates from [8] are applied. Moreover, the order of the templates applied to a quantum circuit results in different costs reductions. However, we use a heuristic approach that the smallest size of templates will be tried last because of applying reconfigured templates using splitting rules. In our experiments, it has also been observed that 3-qubit templates and their corresponding reconfigured templates have been used more frequently than other templates in reducing the quantum gates of benchmark circuits.

References

1. Landauer, R.: Irreversibility and heat generation in the computing process. IBM J. Res. 5, 183–191 (1961)
2. Nielsen, M.A., Chuang, I.L.: Quantum Computation and Quantum Information. Cambridge University Press (2000)
3. Perkowski, M., Lukac, M., Pivtoraiko, M., Kerntopf, P., Folgheraiter, M.: A hierarchicai approach to computer aided design of quantum circuits. In: 6th International Symposium on Representations and Methodology of Future Computing Technology, pp. 201–209 (2003)
4. Miller, D.M., Maslov, D., Dueck, G.W.: A transformation based algorithm for reversible logic synthesis. In: Design Automation Conference (2003)
5. Iwama, K., Kambayashi, Y., Yamashita, S.: Transformation rules for designing CNOT-based quantum circuits. In: Design Automation Conference, New Orleans, Louisiana, USA (2002)
6. Mishchenko, A., Perkowski, M.: Logic synthesis of reversible wave cascades. In: International Workshop on Logic Synthesis (2002)
7. Barenco, A., Bennett, C.H., Cleve, R., DiVinchenzo, D., Margolus, N., Shor, P., Sleator, T., Smolin, J., Weinfurter, H.: Elementary gates for quantum computation. The American Physical Society 52, 3457–3467 (1995)
8. Maslov, D., Young, C., Dueck, G.W., Miller, D.M.: Quantum circuit simplification using templates. In: DATE - Design, Automation and Test in Europe, pp. 1208–1213 (2005)
9. Maslov, D., Dueck, G.W., Miller, D.M.: Toffoli network synthesis with templates. Transactions on Computer Aided Design 24, 807–817 (2005)
10. Hung, W., Song, X., Yang, G., Yang, J., Perkowski, M.: Optimal synthesis of multiple output Boolean functions using a set of quantum gates by symbolic reachability analysis. Transactions on Computer Aided Design 25, 1652–1663 (2006)
11. Große, D., Wille, R., Dueck, G.W., Drechsler, R.: Exact synthesis of elementary quantum gate circuits for reversible functions with don't cares. In: International Symposium on Multiple Valued Logic, pp. 214–219 (2008)
12. Mazder, R.M., Banerjee, A., Dueck, G.W., Pathak, A.: Two-qubit quantum gates to reduce the quantum cost of reversible circuit. In: Proceedings of the International Symposium on Multiple-Valued Logic, pp. 86–92 (2011)
13. Toffoli, T.: Reversible computing. Tech memo MIT/LCS/TM-151, MIT Lab for Comp. Sci. (1980)
14. Peres, A.: Reversible logic and quantum computers. Phys. Rev. A 32, 3266–3276 (1985)
15. Fredkin, E., Toffoli, T.: Conservative logic. International Journal of Theoretical Physics 21, 219–253 (1982)
16. Wille, R., Große, D., Teuber, L., Dueck, G.W., Drechsler, R.: RevLib: An online resource for reversible functions and reversible circuits. In: Int'l Symp. on Multi-Valued Logic, pp. 220–225 (2008), RevLib, http://www.revlib.org
17. Soeken, M., Frehse, S., Wille, R., Drechsler, R.: RevKit: A toolkit for reversible circuit design. In: Workshop on Reversible Computation (2010), RevKit, http://www.revkit.org

Hybrid GF(2) – Boolean Expressions
for Quantum Computing Circuits

Claudio Moraga

European Centre for Soft Computing, 33600 Mieres, Asturias, Spain
Faculty of Computer Science, TU Dortmund University, 44221 Dortmund, Germany
mail@claudio-moraga.eu

Abstract. An extension of Toffoli gates is proposed, that allows them to efficiently realize operations in GF(2) and lattice operations of a Boolean algebra. An equivalent extension is introduced into Reed Muller expressions, including mixed polarities and lattice operations, to support the design of quantum computing circuits with low quantum cost.

Keywords: Quantum Computing, reversible circuits, extensions on Reed Muller expressions.

1   Introduction

Quantum computing represents a model of computation within a sphere –(the Bloch sphere)- in a high dimensional complex Hilbert space. In analogy to classical digital systems, elementary units of information are represented by "quantum bits", (short: qubits). Operations on qubits are done by means of unitary matrices and a computation is a sequence of operations. The Kronecker product of basic operations allows parallel processing of several qubits. Quantum computing "circuits" have a graphical representation based on gates and lines. The lines are not meant to be later realized by "wires". They identify at every stage of a computation, which qubits will be affected by the next elementary operations. The transfer function of a gate is a unitary matrix, as mentioned earlier. Hence, gates satisfy the important requirement of *reversibility*: they have the same number of inputs and outputs, and they realize a bijective function. A quantum computing circuit is reversible if it has the same number of inputs and outputs, it is realized only with fanout free reversible gates, and has no signal feedback. Readers interested in a deeper insight of the fundamentals of reversible and quantum computing may like to refer to some text book (see e.g. [1], [2], [3]).

The basic and possibly most used quantum gates have a support on the set of primitives {EXOR, AND}. An EXOR with only one input is interpreted to denote the negation NOT. If we use the notation (inputs):(outputs) the controlled-NOT, (CNOT) gate realizes $(c, x):(c, c \oplus x)$, where c denotes a control variable and x is the controlled one. It is fairly obvious that if $c = 0$, x does not change and the gate behaves as identity, meanwhile if $c = 1$, x will be complemented since $1 \oplus x = \bar{x}$. The Toffoli gate [4],

A. De Vos and R. Wille (Eds.): RC 2011, LNCS 7165, pp. 54–63, 2012.
© Springer-Verlag Berlin Heidelberg 2012

also called controlled-controlled NOT (CCNOT), realizes $(c_1, c_2, x){:}(\,c_1, c_2, (c_1c_2) \oplus x)$. Notice that setting $x = 1$, the Toffoli gate realizes $(c_1c_2) \oplus 1 = \text{NAND}(c_1, c_2)$. Therefore in a binary world, the Toffoli gate is functionally complete. This may possibly explain why, much effort has been dedicated to optimize Toffoli gates based realizations of quantum circuits.

The present paper intends to be a contribution to improve realizations of Toffoli based quantum circuits, by extending Toffoli gates to accept any number of possibly negated control signals. The well known method of generating Reed Muller expressions to obtain the quantum realization of a given binary function [5], will be extended to work with MPRM expressions of lowest complexity, and to enlarge the GF(2) operations of a Reed Muller expression, with the lattice operations of a Boolean algebra. The name "Hybrid GF(2) – Boolean" has been chosen for the resulting algebraic structures, which allow advantageous realizations with extended Toffoli gates.

2   Hybrid GF(2) – Boolean Expressions

A zero polarity RM expression is basically a GF(2) expression, where all variables appear in a non-complemented form. If the set of operations $\{\oplus, \cdot\}$ is enlarged with complementation, (as independent operation and not as the result of $1 \oplus x$), then other fixed polarities as well as mixed polarities are possible.

The following elementary transformations allow simplifications in the context of MPRM expressions:

(i) $x \oplus xy = x\bar{y}$

If the complexity of a RM expression is measured by counting its terms or, equivalently, by counting the non-zero coefficients of the RM spectrum of the corresponding function, then the above elementary transformation allows a reduction of the complexity of the expression, possibly changing to a mixed polarity (in the case of a larger) expression. The quantum circuits for both expressions are shown in Fig. 1. It is simple to calculate that the quantum cost of directly realizing $x \oplus xy$ is 6, (Since a quantum technology independent realization of a Toffoli gate with a quantum cost of 5 is known [6]), meanwhile the quantum cost of a direct realization of $x\bar{y}$ would amount to 7. This simple observation already points out the fact that the number of terms of a RM expression is not necessarily representative of the quantum cost of its realization.

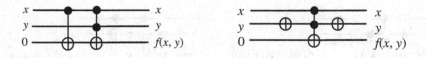

Fig. 1. Realization of $f(x, y) = x \oplus xy$ (left) and $f(x, y) = x\bar{y}$ (right)

(ii) $x \oplus \bar{x}y = y \oplus x\bar{y}$

Let $f(x,y,z) = x \oplus \bar{x}y \oplus x\bar{y}z$. A direct realization, as shown in Fig. 2(a), has a quantum cost of 20. Since $\oplus$ is associative and commutative $f(x,y,z)$ may be expressed as $\bar{x}y \oplus x \oplus x\bar{y}z$ and by using the transformation (i), as $\bar{x}y \oplus x\overline{(\bar{y}z)}$.
This last expression has the realization shown in Fig. 2(b), with a quantum cost of 19. If however instead of using the transformation (i), the transformation (ii) is applied first to $f(x,y,z)$, the expression $y \oplus x\bar{y} \oplus x\bar{y}z$ is obtained; and finally with the transformation (i), $f(x,y,z) = y \oplus x(\bar{y} \cdot \bar{z})$. As shown in Fig. 2(c), this last expression has a realization with a quantum cost of only 15.

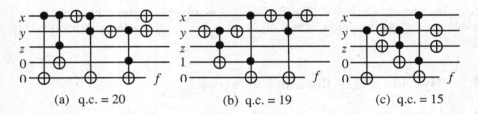

(a)   q.c. = 20   (b)   q.c. = 19   (c)   q.c. = 15

Fig. 2. (a) Direct realization of $f(x,y,z)$; (b) realization after transformation (i); (c) realization after transformation (ii) followed by transformation (i)

(iii) $\bar{x} \oplus \bar{y} = x \oplus y$
　　$\bar{x}y \oplus x\bar{y} = x \oplus y$
　　$x \oplus \bar{y} = \bar{x} \oplus y = 1 \oplus x \oplus y = \overline{(x \oplus y)}$

These simple transformations may also be used to simplify RM expressions and to reduce the quantum cost of their realizations. (See example below).

(iv) $x \oplus y \oplus xy = x \vee y$
　　$1 \oplus x \oplus y \oplus xy = \overline{x \vee y}$
　　$\bar{x} \cdot \bar{y} = \overline{x \vee y}$

This group of transformations relates GF(2) operations with OR/NOR operations of Boolean algebra or makes explicit use of the De Morgan laws. An application of these transformations to optimize the realization of quantum circuits obviously depends on the availability of an efficient OR-Toffoli gate. Such a gate does exist [7] as a slight modification of the seminal quantum Toffoli realization with a cost of 5 introduced by Barenco and colleagues [6]. See Fig. 3.

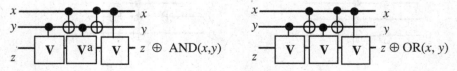

Fig. 3. Left: quantum realization of a Toffoli gate [6] Right: quantum realization of an OR-Toffoli gate [7]

In Fig. 3, $\mathbf{V}$ denotes a unitary matrix such that $\mathbf{V}^2 = \text{NOT}$, and $\mathbf{V}^a$ denotes its adjoint. The control signals to these matrices are x, y and $x \oplus y$. It is easy to see that except when $x = y = 0$, in which case the gate is not activated and realizes an identity, two of the control signals will be 1 and the remaining, 0. In the circuit at the left of Fig. 3, whenever $x \neq y$ one of the $\mathbf{V}$ matrices is activated and the other one is not; $x \oplus y = 1$ and therefore the $\mathbf{V}^a$ matrix is activated and the transfer function of the circuit will be $\mathbf{V} \cdot \mathbf{V}^a$ or $\mathbf{V}^a \cdot \mathbf{V}$. Since $\mathbf{V}$ is unitary, $\mathbf{V} \cdot \mathbf{V}^a = \mathbf{V}^a \cdot \mathbf{V} = \mathbf{I}$. Only when $x = y = 1$, $x \oplus y = 0$; the $\mathbf{V}^a$ matrix will be inhibited, the $\mathbf{V}$ matrices will be active and the transfer function of the circuit will be $\mathbf{V}^2 = \text{NOT}$, controlled by $x = y = 1$. The output of the circuit is therefore $z \oplus xy$, which corresponds to the functionality of a Toffoli gate. In the circuit at the right of Fig. 3, the same analysis indicates that except when $x = y = 0$, two of the $\mathbf{V}$ matrices will be active and the transfer function of the circuit will be $\mathbf{V}^2 = \text{NOT}$, controlled by x or y (or both) equal to 1, giving as output $z \oplus (x \vee y)$. The functionality of the circuit corresponds therefore to an OR-Toffoli gate. It is fairly obvious that both circuits have a quantum cost of 5. If the target qubit is free, then by setting $z = 1$, the circuits would realize $\text{NAND}(x, y)$ and $\text{NOR}(x, y)$, respectively, also with a quantum cost of 5. If the target qubit is not free, then the realization of NAND and NOR would require one additional inverter at the output, and its quantum cost would be 6. Notice however that the last CNOT gate in Fig. 3 left, does not affect the function: it only recovers the value of y, the second control variable. If this CNOT gate is deleted, a Peres gate [8] is obtained, which is also reversible, realizing (x, y, z):$(x, x \oplus y, xy \oplus z)$ and has a quantum cost of 4. Obviously, an OR gate based on a Peres gate has also a quantum cost of 4.

Recall $f(x,y,z) = x \oplus \bar{x}y \oplus x\bar{y}z$, which under transformations (ii) and (i) became $f(x,y,z) = y \oplus x(\bar{y} \cdot \bar{z})$ with a realization as shown in Fig. 2(c) and a quantum cost of 15. If now the last of the transformations (iv) is used, (which is a De Morgan law in the lattice of Boolean algebra), the following is obtained: $f(x,y,z) = y \oplus x(\overline{y \vee z})$. By making use of the above disclosed OR/NOR-Toffoli gate, a realization with a quantum cost of 11 is obtained, as shown in Fig. 4. For the symbolic representation of OR-Toffoli gates, black inverted triangles are used, which are similar to the $\vee$ sign that denotes disjunctions in formal expressions. Since the output of an ancillary line may be considered as garbage, the last gate could be a Peres gate instead of a Toffoli gate, thus reducing the quantum cost to 10.

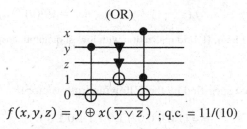

$$f(x,y,z) = y \oplus x(\overline{y \vee z}) \; ; \text{q.c.} = 11/(10)$$

Fig. 4. Hybrid realizations of $f(x,y,z)$ with a quantum cost of 11 or 10

The Barenco-type structure (Fig. 3) allows a further extension of the Toffoli gate to obtain efficient realizations of AND(NOT(x), y) as well as of AND(x, NOT(y)). For these gates, white dots will be used in the schematic representation of the gate, to indicate that an action takes place when the corresponding control variable takes the value 0. Consider the circuit at the left hand side of Fig. 5. Should x be 1, the $\mathbf{V^a}$ gate would be activated. Since either y or $x \oplus y$ will have the value 1, then one of the $\mathbf{V}$ gates will be active and the transfer function of the circuit will be $\mathbf{V \cdot V^a = I}$; therefore the target qubit will not change. On the other hand, if x takes the value 0, then the $\mathbf{V^a}$ gate will be *inhibited*, meanwhile the two $\mathbf{V}$ gates will be activated leading to the desired transfer function $\mathbf{V \cdot V}$ = NOT. Similarly for the circuit at the right hand side of Fig. 5, which was first disclosed in [9]. No explicit complementation of the inhibiting control variable is needed and, therefore, a quantum cost of 5 is obtained. As discussed earlier, Peres based realizations are also possible, having a quantum cost of 4.

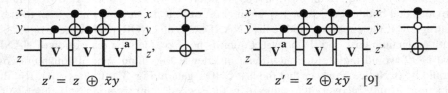

$$z' = z \oplus \bar{x}y \qquad\qquad z' = z \oplus x\bar{y} \quad [9]$$

Fig. 5. Extension of Toffoli gates to be activated by a control variable with value 0

Notice that
$$f(x,y,z) = y \oplus x(\bar{y}\bar{z}) = y \oplus \bar{y}(x\bar{z}) = y \oplus (1 \oplus y)(x\bar{z}) = y \oplus (x\bar{z}) \oplus y(x\bar{z})$$
and, by using the first expression of the (iv) transformation, $f(x,y,z) = y \vee x \cdot \bar{z}$, which has a realization with a quantum cost of 10, as shown in Fig. 6. If the OR gate is based on a Peres gate, the quantum cost is reduced to 9.

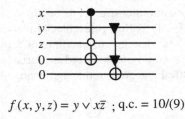

$$f(x,y,z) = y \vee x\bar{z} \; ; \text{q.c.} = 10/(9)$$

Fig. 6. Hybrid realization with lowest quantum cost

Example 1

Let $f(x_3, x_2, x_1, x_0)$ be specified by the following truth vector F:

$$F = [1\,0\,0\,0\,0\,0\,1\,0\,1\,1\,1\,0\,1\,0\,1\,1]^{\mathrm{T}}$$

Let $\otimes$ denote the Kronecker product. The zero-polarity Reed Muller basis is given by:

$$B = [\,1 \ \ x_3\,] \otimes [\,1 \ \ x_2\,] \otimes [\,1 \ \ x_1\,] \otimes [\,1 \ \ x_0\,]$$

$$= [\,1 \ \ x_0 \ \ x_1 \ \ x_1x_0 \ \ x_2 \ \ x_2x_0 \ \ x_2x_1 \ \ x_2x_1x_0 \ \ x_3 \ \ x_3x_0 \ \ x_3x_1 \ \ x_3x_1x_0$$
$$x_3x_2 \ \ x_3x_2x_0 \ \ x_3x_2x_1 \ \ x_3x_2x_1x_0 \ ]$$

For $n = 1$, the Reed Muller transform matrix is $RM_1 = \begin{bmatrix} 1 & 0 \\ 1 & 1 \end{bmatrix}$, corresponding to the numerical values of the basis $[1 \ \ x]$.

For $n = 4$, $RM_4 = RM_1 \otimes RM_1 \otimes RM_1 \otimes RM_1$.

The Reed Muller spectrum of F is calculated as $S_f = RM_4 \cdot F$. It has been shown [10] that a space efficient calculation may be realized as follows:

$$S_f = RM_4 \cdot F = vec(RM_2 \cdot vec^{-1}(F) \cdot (RM_2)^T),$$

where $RM_2 = RM_1 \otimes RM_1$ and vec is a vectorizing operation that chains the columns of a matrix into a column vector. Similarly, vec^{-1} splits a column vector into subvectors, which are ordered as columns of a matrix of a dimension consistent with the matrix operation to be calculated.

Therefore, for the function of the example:

$$S_f = vec\left(\begin{bmatrix} 1 & 0 & 0 & 0 \\ 1 & 1 & 0 & 0 \\ 1 & 0 & 1 & 0 \\ 1 & 1 & 1 & 1 \end{bmatrix} \cdot \begin{bmatrix} 1 & 0 & 1 & 1 \\ 0 & 0 & 1 & 0 \\ 0 & 1 & 1 & 1 \\ 0 & 0 & 0 & 1 \end{bmatrix} \cdot \begin{bmatrix} 1 & 1 & 1 & 1 \\ 0 & 1 & 0 & 1 \\ 0 & 0 & 1 & 1 \\ 0 & 0 & 0 & 1 \end{bmatrix}\right)$$

$$= vec\left(\begin{bmatrix} 1 & 0 & 1 & 1 \\ 1 & 0 & 0 & 1 \\ 1 & 1 & 0 & 0 \\ 1 & 1 & 1 & 1 \end{bmatrix} \cdot \begin{bmatrix} 1 & 1 & 1 & 1 \\ 0 & 1 & 0 & 1 \\ 0 & 0 & 1 & 1 \\ 0 & 0 & 0 & 1 \end{bmatrix}\right) = vec\begin{bmatrix} 1 & 1 & 0 & 1 \\ 1 & 1 & 1 & 0 \\ 1 & 0 & 1 & 0 \\ 1 & 0 & 0 & 0 \end{bmatrix}$$

i.e. $S_f = [\,1 \ 1 \ 1 \ 1 \ 1 \ 1 \ 0 \ 0 \ 0 \ 1 \ 1 \ 0 \ 1 \ 0 \ 0 \ 0\,]^T$

The Reed Muller expression for f is obtained as the inner product $B \cdot S_f$ in GF(2).

$$f(x, y, z) = 1 \oplus x_0 \oplus x_1 \oplus x_1x_0 \oplus x_2 \oplus x_2x_0 \oplus x_3x_0 \oplus x_3x_1 \oplus x_3x_2$$

It is easy to see that this expression has 9 terms, meanwhile the DNF has only 8 minterms. A naïve realization based on the RM expression will achieve a quantum cost of 28 (since for every term with two variables a Toffoli gate (q.c. = 5) and for every single variable, a CNOT gate (q.c. = 1) will be needed). However just by using the associativity, commutativity and distributivity in GF(2) the following expression could be obtained:

$$f(x, y, z) = 1 \oplus (x_1 \oplus x_2)(x_0 \oplus (x_3 \oplus 1)) \oplus x_0(x_3 \oplus 1),$$

and this expression leads to the realization shown in Fig. 7, with a quantum cost of only 14.

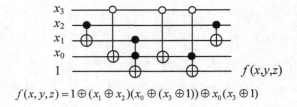

$$f(x, y, z) = 1 \oplus (x_1 \oplus x_2)(x_0 \oplus (x_3 \oplus 1)) \oplus x_0(x_3 \oplus 1)$$

Fig. 7. GF(2) realization of the example function with a quantum cost of 14

If however only the transformation (i) and the distributive law is used, and after that, the transformation (iii) is applied, then an expression with 6 terms is obtained, but a simpler realization is possible, with a quantum cost of 14. See Fig. 8. Notice that the two gates surrounded by a dotted line may be replaced by a single Peres gate and the quantum cost could be further reduced to 12.

$$\begin{aligned}
f(x, y, z) &= (1 \oplus x_0) \oplus (x_1 \oplus x_1 x_0) \oplus (x_2 \oplus x_2 x_0) \oplus x_3 x_0 \oplus x_3 x_1 \oplus x_3 x_2 \\
&= (1 \oplus x_0) \oplus x_1 \bar{x}_0 \oplus x_2 \bar{x}_0 \oplus x_3 x_0 \oplus x_3 x_1 \oplus x_3 x_2 \\
&= (1 \oplus x_0 \oplus x_3 x_0) \oplus (x_1 \oplus x_2) \bar{x}_0 \oplus (x_1 \oplus x_2) x_3 \\
&= (1 \oplus \bar{x}_3 x_0) \oplus (x_1 \oplus x_2)(\bar{x}_0 \oplus x_3) = (1 \oplus \bar{x}_3 x_0) \oplus (x_1 \oplus x_2)(\overline{x_0 \oplus x_3})
\end{aligned}$$

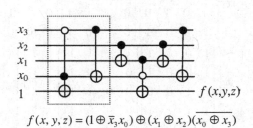

$$f(x, y, z) = (1 \oplus \bar{x}_3 x_0) \oplus (x_1 \oplus x_2)(\overline{x_0 \oplus x_3})$$

Fig. 8. Hybrid realization of the example function with a quantum cost of 14/(12)

The example confirms the early claim that minimizing the number of terms of an expression does not necessarily mean that its realization will achieve minimum quantum cost. More important is proper use of distributivity to obtain a minimum number of products of simple sub-expressions. Hybrid expressions, combining operations in GF(2) with lattice operations of Boolean algebra add flexibility to the search for minimal cost realizations. However, formal methods to obtain and minimize hybrid expressions must still be developed. Small problems may be processed by inspection with the help of the elementary transformations disclosed in Section 2. For larger problems this will not be efficient, if at all possible. However very effective metaheuristics have lately been developed [11], that represent a promising alternative. Moreover, for larger (i.e. more complex) problems, *higher level* extensions of Toffoli/Peres gates, like e.g. symmetric functions might be appropriate [12].

3   Higher Number of Mixed Control Signals

When three or more control variables are used, most authors consider cascading Toffoli gates with two control signals. This simplifies the design, but it requires as many additional ancillary lines as levels in the cascade, minus 1. The quantum cost of the cascade may be optimized if a proper combination of Peres and Toffoli gates is used. Recent results [13] that may be traced back to [6], but obtained in a totally different way, may be adapted to work with mixed control signals [14], as will be shown below. In this case, no additional ancillary lines are required.

Example 2

Low quantum cost design of $f(x_2, x_1, x_0) = x_2\bar{x}_1x_0$

(i) The straight forward approach leads to a realization as shown in Fig. 9, with a quantum cost of 15 and requiring one additional ancillary line.

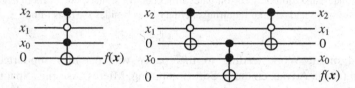

Fig. 9. Cascade realization of a Toffoli gate with three mixed control inputs

Notice that if the upper level gates are chosen to be Peres gates, (to reduce the overall quantum cost by 2), and at the output also the 0 auxiliary input should be recovered, then at the right hand side, the Peres gate would compute

$$x_2\overline{(x_1 \oplus x_2)} = x_2(1 \oplus x_1 \oplus x_2) = x_2 \oplus x_2x_1 \oplus x_2 = x_2x_1.$$

and $x_2\bar{x}_1 \oplus x_2x_1 \neq 0$

A "mirrored" (instead of a straight) Peres gate is needed at the output, to "undo" step by step the processing of the input Peres gate and recover the control variables, as illustrated in Fig. 10. A more detailed analysis may be found in [15].

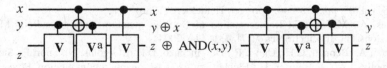

Fig. 10. Quantum model of a Peres gate (left) and of its mirror (right)

(ii) A realization with a quantum cost of 13 and no ancillary lines is shown in Fig. 11, where $\mathbf{W}$ is a unitary matrix such that $\mathbf{W}^4 = \text{NOT}$ and $\mathbf{W} \cdot \mathbf{W}^a = \mathbf{W}^a \cdot \mathbf{W} = \mathbf{I}$, the identity matrix. A formal method to distribute $\mathbf{W}$s and $\mathbf{W}^a$s on the target line to satisfy any mixture of direct and negated control signals is presented in [14]. The method is scalable to any higher number of mixed control signals, reaching a quantum cost of $2^{n+1} - 3$.

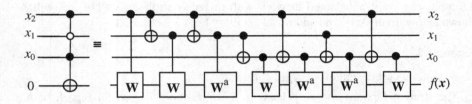

Fig. 11. Optimal realization of a Toffoli gate with 3 control signals, one of them negated, with a quantum cost of 13 and without requiring ancillary lines besides the target line

Acknowledgment. Work leading to this paper was partially supported by the Foundation for the Advancement of Soft Computing, Mieres, Asturias, Spain.

The final version was finished during a Visiting Stay of the author at the Technical University Federico Santa María, Valparaíso, Chile, under the support of the MECE 2 Program for Higher Education, Project Mecesup FSM 0707.

The author thanks the Reviewers for their observations that contributed to improve the original version of the paper.

References

1. Berman, G.P., Doolen, G.D., Mainieri, R., Tsifrinovich, V.I.: Introduction to Quantum Computers. World Scientific, Singapore (1998)
2. Nielsen M.A., Chuang I.L.: Quantum Computation and Quantum Information. Cambridge University Press (2000)
3. Pittenger, A.O.: An Introduction to Quantum Computing Algorithms. Birkhäuser, Boston (2001)
4. Toffoli, T.: Reversible Computing. In: Bakker, J.W., van Leeuwen, J. (eds.) ICALP 1980. LNCS, vol. 85, pp. 632–644. Springer, Heidelberg (1980)
5. Younes, A., Miller, J.F.: Representation of Boolean quantum circuits as Reed Muller expansions. Int. Jr. Electronics 91(7), 431–444 (2004)
6. Barenco, A., Bennett, C.H., Cleve, R., Di Vincenzo, D.P., Margolus, N., Shor, P., Sleator, T., Smolin, J.A., Weinfurter, H.: Elementary gates for quantum computation. Phys- Rev. A 52, 3457–3467 (1995)
7. Moraga, C.: Mixed Polarity Reed Muller expressions and quantum computing. Research Report ECSC-2011-FSC-01, European Centre for Soft Computing (2011)
8. Peres, A.: Reversible logic and quantum computers. Phys. Rev., 3266–3276 (1985)

9. Maslov, D., Dueck, G., Miller, D.M., Negrevergne, C.: Quantum Circuit Simplification and Level Compaction. IEEE Trans. CAD of Integrated Circuits and Systems 27(3), 436–444 (2008)
10. Moraga, C., Stanković, R.S.: On a property of spectral transforms. In: Reed Muller Workshop, pp. 19–26. World Printing Co., Iizuka (2009)
11. Luke, S.: Essentials of Methaheuristics, Lulu (2009), http://cs.gmu.edu/~sean/book/metaheuristics/
12. Hossain, S., Perkowski, M.: The affine gates and affine polarities for quantum arrays with small cost. In: 17th Int. Workshop on Post-Binary ULSI Systems, pp. 25–34 (2008)
13. Sasanian, Z., Miller, D.M.: Transforming MCT circuits to NCVW circuits. In: 3rd Workshop on Reversible Computation, Gent, Belgium, pp. 163–174. Press University of Bremen (2011)
14. Moraga, C.: Low quantum cost realization of Toffoli gates with multiple mixed control signals. Research Report FSC-2011-08, European Centre for Soft Computing, Mieres, Spain (2011)
15. Maslov, D., Dueck, G.W.: Improved quantum cost for n-bit Toffoli gates. Electronic Letters 39(25), 1790–1791 (2003)

RevKit: An Open Source Toolkit
for the Design of Reversible Circuits

Mathias Soeken[1], Stefan Frehse[1], Robert Wille[1], and Rolf Drechsler[1,2]

[1] Institute of Computer Science, University of Bremen, 28359 Bremen, Germany
[2] Cyber-Physical Systems, DFKI GmbH, 28359 Bremen, Germany
revkit@informatik.uni-bremen.de
http://www.revkit.org

Abstract. In recent years, research in the domain of reversible circuit design has attracted significant attention leading to many different approaches e.g. for synthesis, optimization, simulation, verification, and test. The open source toolkit RevKit is an attempt to make these developments publicly available to other researchers. For this purpose, a modular and extendable framework has been provided which easily enables the addition of new methods and tools.

In this paper, we introduce the functionality as well as the internals of RevKit. We provide examples and use cases showing how to apply RevKit and its components in order to create and execute customized design flows. Furthermore, we demonstrate how the architecture and the design concepts of RevKit can be exploited to easily develop new or improved methods for reversible circuit design.

1 Introduction

The development of computing machines has found great success in the last decades. Nowadays billions of components are built on a few square centimeters – and this increasing trend continues. The number of transistors in an integrated circuit doubles every 18 months – also known as *Moore's Law*. However, it is obvious that such an exponential growth must reach its limits in the future. Otherwise, the miniaturization would reach a level where transistors consist of only single atoms. Furthermore, power dissipation more and more becomes a crucial issue for designing high performance digital circuits.

To further satisfy the need for more computational power, alternatives are required that go beyond the scope of the conventional (CMOS) technologies. Reversible logic marks a promising new direction where all operations are performed in an invertible manner. That is, in contrast to conventional logic, only bijective operations are allowed implying a reversible computation, i.e. the inputs can be obtained from the outputs *and* vice versa. This reversibility builds the basis for emerging technologies that may replace, or at least enhance, conventional computer chips, e.g. in the domain of low-power design [1,2,3], quantum computation [4,5,6], optical computing [7], DNA computing [8], as well as nanotechnologies [9].

A. De Vos and R. Wille (Eds.): RC 2011, LNCS 7165, pp. 64–76, 2012.

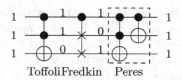

ToffoliFredkin   Peres

Fig. 1. Reversible gates

The basic concepts of reversible logic are not new and were already introduced in the 60's by Landauer [1] and further refined by Bennett [2] and Toffoli [10]. They observed that due to the reversibility fanouts and feedback are not directly allowed in reversible circuits. As a consequence new libraries of (reversible) gates have been introduced including e.g. Toffoli gates [10], Fredkin gates [11], and Peres gates [12]. Figure 1 shows these gates in a cascade. Each gate consists of control lines (denoted by ●) and target lines (denoted by ⊕ except for the Fredkin gate where an ✕ is used instead). For a Toffoli gate, the value of the target line becomes inverted, if all control lines are assigned to the logic value 1 while for the Fredkin gate the target lines are interchanged in this case. The Peres gate is a cascade of two Toffoli gates. The annotated values in Fig. 1 demonstrate the computation of the respective gates. As can be seen, the calculation can be done in both directions, i.e. it is reversible.

Even if this represents the basis for research in the area of reversible circuits, the topic was not intensively studied by computer scientists before the year 2000. The main reason for that may be due to the fact that applications of such circuits have been seen as "dreams of the future". However, this changed with recently made achievements. For example, in the domain of low-power design, first reversible circuits have been built which are powered by their input signals only and do not need additional power supplies (see e.g. [3]). In quantum computation, factorization has been solved in polynomial time whereas only exponential solving methods are known for conventional circuits (see e.g. [4,6]). These achievements (together with others) significantly moved the topic forward so that nowadays reversible logic is seen as a promising research area. As a consequence, in the last years computer scientists started to develop new methods for the design of reversible circuits. Among others, these include approaches for synthesis (see e.g. [13,14,15]), optimization (see e.g. [14]), simulation (e.g. [16]), verification (e.g. [17,18,19]), and test (e.g. [20,21]).

However, most of the resulting methods are not publicly available[1]. This often makes the development of new methods harder since e.g. previous approaches are not available for comparison. Furthermore, approaches have to be re-implemented from scratch in order to modify or improve them. The lack of tools for reversible hardware design makes it hard for beginners to get involved in the topic.

---

[1] Exceptions are e.g. the RMRLS synthesis approach [22] which is available at `http://www.princeton.edu/~cad/projects.html` or the quantum simulator QuIDDPro [16] which is available at `http://vlsicad.eecs.umich.edu/Quantum/qp/`

The open source toolkit RevKit is an attempt to make these developments publicly available to other researchers. For this purpose, a modular and extendable framework has been provided which easily enables the addition of new methods and tools. Besides basic functionality (like parser and export functions), RevKit already provides elaborated methods for synthesis, optimization, and verification. In this sense, RevKit addresses users who simply want to apply the framework and its tools as well as developers who actively want to develop further methods on top of the framework. For this purpose, RevKit is available online at http://www.revkit.org.

In this paper, we introduce the functionality as well as the internals of RevKit. We provide examples and use cases showing how to apply RevKit and its components in order to create and execute customized design flows. The paper is structured as follows. First, RevKit and the main approaches are briefly reviewed in the next section. Section 3 illustrates the application of RevKit by means of the Python interface and by means of a graphical user interface. Afterwards, the the architecture as well as the design concepts of RevKit are introduced in Sect. 4 enabling to easily extend or improve the framework with further functionality. Section 5 concludes the paper.

2   The RevKit Framework

RevKit is an open source toolkit available at www.revkit.org which aims to make recent developments in the domain of reversible circuit design accessible to other researchers. It provides core functionality like read-in routines for functions and reversible circuits (based on the RevLib format introduced in [23]), several export functions (again into the RevLib format, but LATEX and BLIF dumps are also available), cost calculations, and more. Furthermore, more elaborated methods for synthesis, optimization, and verification of reversible (and quantum) circuits are available including:

Synthesis
- A transformation-based method inspired by the concepts of [24] and the extension based on the Reed Muller spectra [25]
- The BDD-based synthesis method as introduced in [15]
- The KFDD-based synthesis method as introduced in [26]
- The heuristic synthesis with output permutation method as introduced in [27]
- The ESOP-based synthesis method inspired by the concepts of [28]
- The exact synthesis method as introduced in [29]

Optimization
- The window optimization method as introduced in [30]
- The circuit line reduction method as introduced in [31]
- The adding lines optimization method as introduced in [32]

Verification
- The SAT-based equivalence checker as introduced in [19]

Further Methods
- A naïve method to embed irreversible functions into reversible ones (needed e.g. to synthesize irreversible functions using the transformation-based method)
- A simple simulation engine (for reversible circuits working on Boolean values)
- A simple decomposition method that maps a given reversible circuit (composed of Toffoli, Fredkin, and Peres gates) to its equivalent quantum circuit (composed of NOT, CNOT, V, and V+ gates) inspired by the concepts of [33] and [34]
- Support of hierarchical circuitry (i.e. modules, flattening of circuits, etc.), sequential circuits, annotations, and more
- Visualization of circuits

All these tools and algorithms are written in C++ and directly accessible by an API. That is, they can be used in other C++ programs. Furthermore, all functions are also exposed as a Python library² as well as in a graphical user interface. This enables the user to create and execute customized design flows as illustrated in the next sections.

3   The Users' Perspective: Applying RevKit

Accessing the API of RevKit using C++ requires to write fully executable C++ programs which need to be compiled after every modification. In particular when using the toolkit for the purpose of evaluation and experimentation, this work flow is very inflexible.

To overcome this limitation, RevKit offers bindings of all functions and algorithms either to the Python language or to a graphical user interface. This allows to utilize RevKit without re-compilation. At the same time, the high performance of the algorithms is exploited since both, the Python binding as well as the graphical user interface, directly invoke the respective assembly code.

3.1   Using the Python Interface

In this section, the advantages of the Python bindings are demonstrated by means of two use cases. First, an interactive application of the Python shell is outlined. Afterwards, it is shown how to utilize the expressive Python syntax in order to create compact scripts defining a customized design flow.

Interactive Application in the Python Shell. A Python shell can be utilized enabling a dynamic interaction with the RevKit functions and algorithms. Furthermore, sophisticated Python shells such as *IPython* [35] additionally allow syntax highlighting, tab completion, UNIX shell interaction, and integrated documentation.

---

² For this purpose, the Boost.Python library was utilized. For further information visit http://www.boost.org/doc/libs/1_47_0/libs/python/doc/index.html

```
$ ipython
In [1]: from revkit import *
In [2]: circ = circuit(2)
In [3]: append_not(circ, 0)
Out[3]: <revkit_python.gate object at 0xb7348454>
In [4]: append_cnot(circ, 0, 1)
Out[4]: <revkit_python.gate object at 0xb734848c>
In [5]: circ
Out[5]:
O*
-O
In [6]: init_gui()
Out[6]: <PyQt4.QtGui.QApplication object at 0xb72be26c>
In [7]: w = display_circuit(circ)
In [8]: w.simulate([False, True])
```

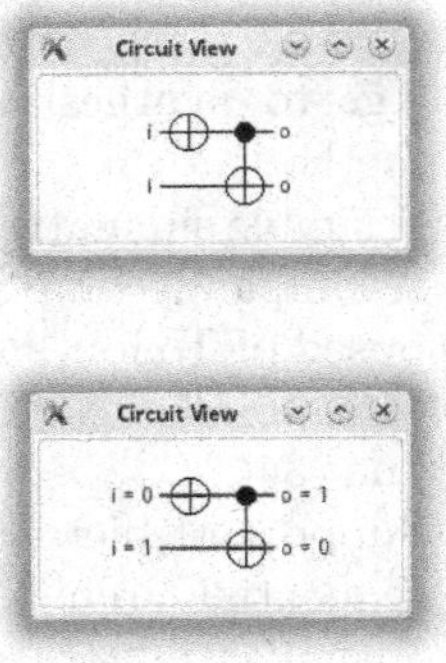

Fig. 2. Command line interface

As an example, consider the command line flow as outlined in Fig. 2. After the RevKit library is imported (see Command 1), a circuit consisting of a NOT and a CNOT gate is created (see Command 2 for the initialization of the circuit as well as Command 3 and Command 4 for the addition of the gates). Then, the resulting circuit is printed out on the console (Command 5), displayed in the GUI (Command 7), and simulated (Command 8). For this purpose, the last two commands open the GUI as shown on the right-hand side of Fig. 2.

Overall, using RevKit in the Python shell, the user directly gets feedback for the invoked actions. Thus, it is ideal e.g. for a first examination in order to observe the behavior of different design flows.

Python Scripts. An alternative to the interactive application is the use of scripts. They enable e.g. to define sequences of commands that, afterwards, can be executed on several instances, several times, or with different parameters.

As an example, Fig. 3 shows a Python script that creates an incrementer circuit and verifies it using exhaustive simulation. After importing the RevKit Python library (Line 3), a helper function is defined which maps a list of Boolean numbers to its natural representation (Line 5). The syntax can almost directly be mapped to the formula $\sum_{b_i} b_i \cdot 2^i$ for a $b = (b_0 \dots b_{n-1})$. The size of the circuit is configurable by a program argument and defined in Line 7. The incrementer structure of the circuit is built in Lines 8 and 9 by prepending a gate with a target on line c and control lines on all preceding lines. In order to verify the correctness of this circuit, the truth table of it is created (Line 11/12). Then, for each line of the truth table it is checked whether it adheres the specification (Line 13). More precisely, it is checked whether adding 1 to each input value results in the desired output value. In case the script generates no output, the verification was successful. Otherwise, an assertion is thrown which can be further inspected, e.g. by checking the respective values for the variables _in and _out.

```
1   #!/usr/bin/python
2   import sys
3   from revkit import *
4
5   def b2d(bits): return sum([b * 2**i for i, b in enumerate(bits)])
6
7   n = int(sys.argv[1])
8   circ = circuit(n)
9   for c in range(n): prepend_toffoli(circ, range(c), c)
10
11  spec = binary_truth_table()
12  circuit_to_truth_table(circ, spec)
13  for [_in, _out] in spec.entries: assert((b2d(_in) + 1) % 2**n == b2d(_out))
```

Fig. 3. Python script

Overall, using the RevKit bindings and the syntactical features of Python, scripts also for complex tasks can be written within few lines of code.

3.2 Using the Graphical User Interface

Besides the Python library, also a *graphical user interface* (GUI) is available in RevKit. This enables the creation and execution of customized design flows without writing any line of code. Instead, the respective steps of a design flow to be executed can easily put together by means of blocks to be connected by a graph. Each block performs an operation and may have ports for the respective input parameters and output results. Input ports can be connected to output ports forming a channel when they support the same data types.

As an example, a *Circuit from file* block reads a circuit from a given file-name and passes the resulting data-structure to its single output port of type *Circuit*. Then, this block can be connected to a *Line Reduction* block which takes this circuit as a parameter and performs the line reduction approach [31]. Afterwards, the result is provided at the output port of this block. In this manner, more complex scenarios can be set up.

When executing the design flow, the graph is sorted in a topologically order and is executed level wise. Visual feedback provides the user with current progress information, i.e. which steps have already been performed and which step is currently being executed. In the following, two use cases illustrating possible applications of the RevKit GUI are presented.

Building Custom Design Flows. An example flow is given in Fig. 4. Here, a reversible function given as truth table is synthesized utilizing a heuristic [24] as well as an exact [29] approach. Afterwards, the resulting circuits are checked for equivalence. Besides that, the results of each synthesis run are passed to a statistics element which provides information e.g. about the circuit cost and also visualizes the circuit.

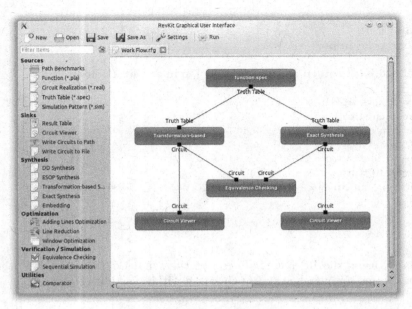

Fig. 4. Example GUI execution

Benchmarking. The elementary blocks in the RevKit GUI are of different complexity. While some provide very basic operations such as parsing files, more powerful blocks exist. As an example, the block *RevLib Functions* provides access to the RevLib [23] database. A respective block is depicted in its expanded form in Fig. 5. The table on the left-hand side lists all benchmarks that meet certain criteria specified on the right-hand side, i.e. functions with more than 5 but less than 8 inputs as well as functions with more than 3 outputs. When executing this block, all these functions can be passed to the successive blocks. Therewith, a whole set of functions can sequentially be applied e.g. to a synthesis approach. The results of such a process can afterwards be collected in another block which enables to export a result table in terms of a CSV or LaTeX file.

4 The Developers' Perspective: Extending RevKit

Besides providing tools and algorithms, RevKit also aims to support researchers in the development of new or improved methods for reversible circuit design. To this end, RevKit is based on a very modular and extendable framework which is introduced in more detail in this section. First, the architecture of RevKit is described followed by a brief discussion of applied design concepts. Afterwards, it is illustrated, by means of an example, how new approaches can be added to the framework.

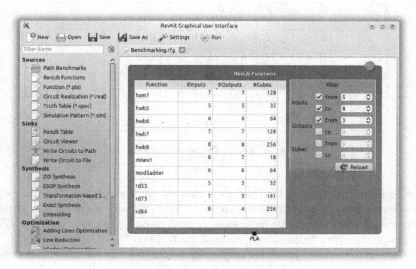

Fig. 5. Benchmarking example

4.1   Architecture and Design Concepts

The architecture of RevKit is briefly illustrated in Fig. 6. As can be seen, RevKit consists of three main parts:

– the core, which provides data-structures (e.g. to store functions or circuits) and basic functionality (like parsing routines, export functions, cost calculations, circuit modifications) which can be used by every algorithm,
– the respective approaches and methods for reversible circuit design (e.g. synthesis, optimization, or verification), and
– the different applications built on top of the framework (e.g. the generic usage by means of the Python bindings or a precise application that combines some algorithms in a certain way).

Additionally, RevKit makes use of third-party libraries like e.g. the *Colorado University Decision Diagram Package* (CUDD) [36], the metaSMT framework [37], and some C++-libraries.

The core and the corresponding algorithms form the main implementation of the framework. The respective algorithms are completely independent from each other, but rely on generic interfaces. In doing so, it is possible to utilize existing methods without a detailed treatment of them. For example, if a new optimization approach based on re-synthesis is added, the respective synthesis calls would be invoked by the generic interface. At run-time (or in a precise application), the respective synthesis approach can then be chosen by parameters (denoted by the dashed arrow in Fig. 6). This enables a huge flexibility since the new optimization approach does not only rely on one single synthesis method, but can exploit all available ones. This also includes synthesis approaches that

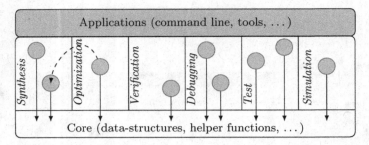

Fig. 6. Architecture of RevKit

will be added in the future. Furthermore, this modular structure (together with the interfaces) has the advantage that newly added methods do not affect already implemented functionality. In fact, even removing one approach will not affect the overall framework from compiling and operating.

Besides that, being prepared for future developments was an important design criterion during the implementation of RevKit. This can be illustrated very well by the support of the respective gate libraries for the considered circuits. So far, RevKit supports the established Toffoli gate, the Fredkin gate, and the Peres gate as well as the quantum V gate and the quantum V+ gate. However, in the future other gate types may be used. This would not only affect the data-structures of RevKit, but would also have implications for many approaches like simulation or verification. In order to keep RevKit flexible, generic structures are applied as well. More precisely, a generic data-structure including a so called target tag is used. These target tags can be defined separately without modifying the core of the framework. Having these target tags, new gate types can be easily supported by extending or overriding the concerned methods. For example, in the case of simulation, only the treatment of a single gate has to be extended while the overall simulation engine can remain unaltered.

The usage of these design concepts ensures a high extendability of the framework. Furthermore, several scripts are provided to aid developers in creating new algorithms from scratch. In particular, they generate basic code skeletons in order to allow an easy integration of new approaches and to make existing algorithms accessible. The next section illustrates this by means of an example.

4.2   Adding a New Approach to RevKit

Figure 7 shows the complete source code of an optimization approach that can be added to RevKit in this form. In fact, a window optimization approach is realized, where sub-circuits are considered from left to right. In each iteration, the currently considered sub-circuit is re-synthesized. If a sub-circuit with smaller cost results, the newly generated sub-circuit is substituted with the original one.

In the first lines of Fig. 7, the respective parameters are given, i.e. the resulting circuit (*circ*), the original circuit (*base*), and some settings (*settings*), which are parsed into local variables in Lines 4–7. As can be seen, the simulation and the

```
 1  bool window_optimization(circuit& circ, const circuit& base,
 2      properties::ptr settings)
 3  {
 4    unsigned window_length = get(settings, "window_length");
 5    simulation_func simulation = get(settings, "simulation");
 6    truth_table_synthesis_func synthesis = get(settings, "synthesis");
 7    cost_function cf = get(settings, "cost_function");
 8
 9    unsigned pos = 0u;
10    while (pos < base.num_gates())
11    {
12      unsigned length = std::min(
13          window_length, base.num_gates() - pos);
14      unsigned to = pos + length;
15
16      subcircuit s(base, pos, to);
17
18      binary_truth_table spec;
19      circuit_to_truth_table(s, spec, simulation);
20
21      circuit new_part;
22      bool ok = synthesis(new_part, spec);
23
24      bool cheaper = ok && costs(new_part, cf) < costs(s, cf);
25
26      append_circuit(circ, cheaper ? new_part : s);
27
28      pos = to;
29    }
30
31    return true;
32  }
```

Fig. 7. Sources for a simple optimization approach

synthesis approach are passed by settings and stored in respective variables. As discussed above, this employs a generic interface, i.e. no concrete simulation or synthesis approach is invoked but defined from outside when calling the window optimization algorithm. Then, the original circuit is traversed from left to right (Line 10) and a sub-circuit of a certain size (defined in the settings) is extracted and stored in s (Lines 12–16). Afterwards, the function of the considered sub-circuit is extracted (Lines 18–19) and passed to the synthesis approach (Lines 21–22). Finally, the costs of the sub-circuits are compared in Line 24 (using a cost function again specified in the settings). If the newly synthesized sub-circuit is cheaper than the original one, then this new one is appended to the resulting circuit. Otherwise, the original sub-circuit is used (Line 26).

As can be seen, using RevKit this approach can be implemented in a very compact and straight-forward way. Existing approaches (in this case synthesis methods) are utilized. Furthermore, the resulting approach is very flexible since both, the synthesis method and the considered cost function, can be arbitrarily selected.

5 Conclusions

In this paper, we reviewed the functionality as well as the internals of RevKit and provided examples and use cases showing how to apply RevKit and its components in order to design reversible circuits. For this purpose, several interfaces provided by RevKit (Python bindings, the graphical user interface, or the C++-API) can be exploited. RevKit itself as well as further documentation is available at www.revkit.org.

Acknowledgments. This work was supported by the German Research Foundation (DFG) (DR 287/20-1).

References

1. Landauer, R.: Irreversibility and Heat Generation in the Computing Process. IBM Journal of Research and Development 5(3), 183–191 (1961)
2. Bennett, C.H.: Logical Reversibility of Computation. IBM Journal of Research and Development 17(6), 525–532 (1973)
3. Desoete, B., DeVos, A.: A reversible carry-look-ahead adder using control gates. Integration 33(1-2), 89–104 (2002)
4. Shor, P.W.: Algorithms for Quantum Computation: Discrete Logarithms and Factoring. In: Symp. on Foundations of Computer Science, pp. 124–134. IEEE Computer Society (November 1994)
5. Nielsen, M.A., Chuang, I.L.: Quantum Computation and Quantum Information. Cambridge University Press, New York (2000)
6. Vandersypen, L.M.K., Steffen, M., Breyta, G., Yannoni, C.S., Sherwood, M.H., Chuang, I.L.: Nature 414, 883–887 (2001)
7. Cuykendall, R., Andersen, D.R.: Reversible optical computing circuits. Optical Letters 12(7), 542–544 (1987)
8. Thapliyal, H., Srinivas, M.B.: The need of DNA computing: Reversible designs of adders and multipliers using Fredkin gate. In: Proceedings of SPIE, vol. 6050 (December 2005)
9. Merkle, R.C.: Reversible electronic logic using switches. Nanotechnology 4(1), 21–40 (1993)
10. Toffoli, T.: Reversible Computing. In: de Bakker, J.W., van Leeuwen, J. (eds.) ICALP 1980. LNCS, vol. 85, pp. 632–644. Springer, Heidelberg (1980)
11. Fredkin, E., Toffoli, T.: Conservative logic. Int'l. Journal of Theoretical Physics 21(3), 219–253 (1982)
12. Peres, A.: Reversible logic and quantum computers. Phys. Rev. A 32(6), 3266–3276 (1985)
13. Shende, V., Prasad, A., Markov, I., Hayes, J.: Synthesis of reversible logic circuits. IEEE Trans. on CAD 22(6), 710–722 (2003)

14. Maslov, D., Dueck, G.W., Miller, D.M.: Toffoli network synthesis with templates. IEEE Trans. on CAD 24(6), 807–817 (2005)
15. Wille, R., Drechsler, R.: BDD-based synthesis of reversible logic for large functions. In: Design Automation Conference, pp. 270–275. ACM (July 2009)
16. Viamontes, G.F., Markov, I.L., Hayes, J.P.: Quantum Circuit Simulation. Springer, Heidelberg (2009)
17. Viamontes, G.F., Markov, I.L., Hayes, J.P.: Checking equivalence of quantum circuits and states. In: Int'l Conf. on Computer-Aided Design, pp. 69–74. IEEE (November 2007)
18. Gay, S.J., Nagarajan, R., Papanikolaou, N.: QMC: A Model Checker for Quantum Systems. In: Gupta, A., Malik, S. (eds.) CAV 2008. LNCS, vol. 5123, pp. 543–547. Springer, Heidelberg (2008)
19. Wille, R., Große, D., Miller, D.M., Drechsler, R.: Equivalence Checking of Reversible Circuits. In: Int'l. Symp. on Multiple-Valued Logic, 324–330. IEEE Computer Society (May 2009)
20. Polian, I., Fiehn, T., Becker, B., Hayes, J.P.: A Family of Logical Fault Models for Reversible Circuits. In: Asian Test Symposium, pp. 422–427. IEEE Computer Society (December 2005)
21. Patel, K.N., Hayes, J.P., Markov, I.L.: Fault testing for reversible circuits. IEEE Trans. on CAD 23(8), 1220–1230 (2004)
22. Gupta, P., Agrawal, A., Jha, N.K.: An Algorithm for Synthesis of Reversible Logic Circuits. IEEE Trans. on CAD of Integrated Circuits and Systems 25(11), 2317–2330 (2006)
23. Wille, R., Große, D., Teuber, L., Dueck, G.W., Drechsler, R.: RevLib: An Online Resource for Reversible Functions and Reversible Circuits. In: Int'l Symp. on Multiple-Valued Logic, pp. 220–225 (May 2008)
24. Miller, D.M., Maslov, D., Dueck, G.W.: A transformation based algorithm for reversible logic synthesis. In: Design Automation Conference, pp. 318–323. ACM (June 2003)
25. Maslov, D., Dueck, G.W., Miller, D.M.: Techniques for the synthesis of reversible Toffoli networks. ACM Trans. Design Autom. Electr. Syst. 12(4), 42:1–42:28 (2007)
26. Soeken, M., Wille, R., Drechsler, R.: Hierarchical synthesis of reversible circuits using positive and negative Davio decomposition. In: Int'l Design and Test Workshop, pp. 143–148 (December 2010)
27. Wille, R., Große, D., Dueck, G.W., Drechsler, R.: Reversible Logic Synthesis with Output Permutation. In: Int'l Conf. on VLSI Design, pp. 189–194. IEEE (January 2009)
28. Fazel, K., Thornton, M., Rice, J.: ESOP-based Toffoli Gate Cascade Generation. In: IEEE Pacific Rim Conf. on Communications, Computers and Signal Processing, pp. 206–209. IEEE (August 2007)
29. Große, D., Wille, R., Dueck, G.W., Drechsler, R.: Exact Multiple-Control Toffoli Network Synthesis With SAT Techniques. IEEE Trans. on CAD 28(5), 703–715 (2009)
30. Soeken, M., Wille, R., Dueck, G.W., Drechsler, R.: Window optimization of reversible and quantum circuits. In: Int'l Symp. on Design and Diagnostics of Electronic Circuits and Systems, pp. 341–345 (April 2010)
31. Wille, R., Soeken, M., Drechsler, R.: Reducing the number of lines in reversible circuits. In: Design Automation Conference, pp. 647–652. ACM (June 2010)
32. Miller, D.M., Wille, R., Drechsler, R.: Reducing reversible circuit cost by adding lines. In: Int'l Symp. on Multiple-Valued Logic, pp. 217–222 (May 2010)

33. Barenco, A., Bennett, C.H., Cleve, R., DiVincenzo, D.P., Margolus, N., Shor, P., Sleator, T., Smolin, J.A., Weinfurter, H.: Elementary gates for quantum computation. Phys. Rev. A 52(5), 3457–3467 (1995)
34. Maslov, D., Dueck, G.: Improved quantum cost for n-bit toffoli gates. Electronics Letters 39(25), 1790–1791 (2003)
35. Pérez, F., Granger, B.E.: Ipython: A system for interactive scientific computing. Computing in Science and Engineering 9(3), 21–29 (2007)
36. Somenzi, F.: CUDD: CU Decision Diagram Package Release 2.3.1. University of Colorado at Boulder (2001), CUDD, `vlsi.colorado.edu/~fabio/CUDD/`
37. Haedicke, F., Frehse, S., Fey, G., Große, D., Drechsler, R.: metaSMT: Focus on Your Application not on Solver Integration. In: Int'l Workshop on Design and Implementation of Formal Tools and Systems (November 2011)

Transforming MCT Circuits to NCVW Circuits

Zahra Sasanian and D. Michael Miller*

Department of Computer Science, University of Victoria
Victoria, BC, Canada V8W 3P6
{sasanian,mmiller}@uvic.ca

Abstract. Mapping a circuit of reversible gates to a circuit of elementary quantum gates is a key step in synthesizing quantum realizations of Boolean functions. The library containing NOT, controlled-NOT and controlled square-root-of-NOT gates has been considered extensively. In this paper, we extend the library to include fourth-root-of-NOT gates. Experimental results using REVLIB benchmark circuits show that using this extended library results in smaller quantum circuits.

1 Introduction

Many reversible circuit synthesis methods have been presented in the literature. A good review can be found in [10]. Most methods produce a circuit composed of a cascade of basic reversible gates. After, or sometimes during, synthesis the reversible gates are mapped to elementary quantum gates implemented in the target technology, a step analogous to technology-mapping in traditional digital circuit design. Much of the work in this area has focused on the quantum gate library of NOT, controlled-NOT, controlled-V and controlled-V^+ gates, which is termed the NCV library. The last two are *square-root-of-NOT* gates. The work here extends the library to include controlled-W and controlled-W^+ gates which are *fourth-root-of-NOT* gates. The question we seek to address is to what extent the NCVW library will yield smaller quantum circuits.

Although the paper concentrates on MCT reversible gates, the proposed methods can be applied to other reversible gates, *e.g.* Fredkin [2] gates, by transforming them to Toffoli gate realizations. The approach can also be targeted to other quantum gate libraries.

All circuits described in this paper have been verified using the QMDD circuit equivalence checker described in [11]. The NCV and NCVW catalogs of circuit realizations for MCT gates, the programs that generate those catalogs and the MCT to quantum circuit mapping program (in Python) are available from the authors.

The rest of the paper is organized as follows. Section 2 gives the necessary background. Section 3 outlines an approach to finding NCVW realizations of single MCT gates, and Section 4 shows how that work can be used in finding

---

* This work was supported in part by a Discovery Grant from the Natural Sciences and Engineering Research Council of Canada.

A. De Vos and R. Wille (Eds.): RC 2011, LNCS 7165, pp. 77–88, 2012.

NCVW realizations of MCT circuits. Experimental results are given in Section 5 and the paper finishes with conclusions and suggestions for ongoing work in Section 6.

2   Background

We here present the background necessary for this paper. Readers interested in a more detailed introduction should consult the literature.

Definition 1. *A multiple-output Boolean function is* **reversible** *if it maps each input assignment to a unique output assignment.*

A reversible function is realized by a cascade of reversible gates with no fan-out or feedback [5]. A completely or incompletely-specified irreversible function can be embedded into a reversible function, usually with more inputs and outputs, and then realized by a reversible circuit [3].

Definition 2. *A* **multiple-control Toffoli** *(MCT) gate with* **target line** x_j *and* **control lines** $\{x_{i_1}, x_{i_2} \cdots x_{i_k}\}$, *maps* $(x_1 \ldots x_j \ldots x_n)$ *to*

$$(x_1 \ldots (x_{i_1} x_{i_2} \cdots x_{i_k}) \oplus x_j \ldots x_n).$$

Note that all controls must be 1 for the target to be inverted. An MCT gate with no control is the well-known **NOT** *gate. An MCT gate with a single control line is called a* **controlled-NOT** *(CNOT) gate. We use $T(C; t)$ to denote the MCT gate with C being the set of controls and t being the target.*

Note that for all circuits considered in this work, MCT gate controls and controls for the quantum gates discussed below must have binary (0 or 1) and not quantum values.

Fredkin gates [2], Peres and inverse-Peres gates [6] are also used in reversible circuits. Each such gate can be substituted by an equivalent sequence of MCT gates. Indeed, any reversible gate can be substituted by a sequence of MCT gates. A reversible circuit composed of only MCT gates is thus used as the starting point for the approach presented in this paper.

Many quantum gates have been defined and studied in the literature [5]. Here we consider what we term the NCVW library which consist of the NOT and $CNOT$ gates given above and four single-control gates (V, V^+, W, W^+) defined below.

It is well known (see [5] for details) that the operation of each gate in an n-line reversible or quantum circuit can be represented by a square matrix of dimension 2^n. The construction of the matrix depends on which line is the target, which lines are the control(s) and a 2×2 matrix defining the operation on the target line. For example, the target matrix for an MCT gate, including NOT and $CNOT$, is $\mathbf{N} = \begin{pmatrix} 0 & 1 \\ 1 & 0 \end{pmatrix}$.

Theorem 1. *Consider the matrix*

$$\mathbf{R}_k = \frac{1}{2} \begin{pmatrix} 1 + i^{2/k} & 1 - i^{2/k} \\ 1 - i^{2/k} & 1 + i^{2/k} \end{pmatrix} \qquad (1)$$

where k is a power of 2. $\mathbf{R}_k$ is a k-th root of $\mathbf{N}$, i.e. $(\mathbf{R}_k)^k = \mathbf{N}$.

Proof: Consider

$$\mathbf{R}_p \times \mathbf{R}_p = \frac{1}{2} \begin{pmatrix} 1 + i^{2/p} & 1 - i^{2/p} \\ 1 - i^{2/p} & 1 + i^{2/p} \end{pmatrix} \times \frac{1}{2} \begin{pmatrix} 1 + i^{2/p} & 1 - i^{2/p} \\ 1 - i^{2/p} & 1 + i^{2/p} \end{pmatrix} \qquad (2)$$

$$= \frac{1}{2} \begin{pmatrix} 1 + i^{4/p} & 1 - i^{4/p} \\ 1 - i^{4/p} & 1 + i^{4/p} \end{pmatrix} \qquad (3)$$

The matrix in Equation 3 is $\mathbf{R}_{p/2}$ which is verified by setting $k = p/2$ in Equation 1. Since $\mathbf{R}_p \times \mathbf{R}_p = \mathbf{R}_{p/2}$ and $\mathbf{R}_1 = \mathbf{N}$, it follows by induction that for k a power of 2, $(\mathbf{R}_k)^k = \mathbf{N}$. $\qquad \square$

Corollary 1.1 Since the conjugate of the product of two matrices is the product of their conjugates, $(\overline{\mathbf{R}}_k)^k = \mathbf{N}$.

Let $\mathbf{V} = \mathbf{R}_2 = \frac{1}{2} \begin{pmatrix} 1+i & 1-i \\ 1-i & 1+i \end{pmatrix}$. Clearly, $\mathbf{V} \times \mathbf{V} = \mathbf{N}$. Let $\mathbf{V}^+$ be the conjugate transpose (adjoint) of $\mathbf{V}$. It follows from Corollary 1.1 that $\mathbf{V}^+ \times \mathbf{V}^+ = \mathbf{N}$. further, it is readily verified that $\mathbf{V}^+ = \mathbf{V}^{-1}$.

Definition 3. *A **controlled-V** gate applies the transformation defined by the matrix $\mathbf{V}$ when the single control line has value 1. Likewise, a **controlled-V$^+$** gate applies the transformation defined by the matrix $\mathbf{V}^+$ when the single control line has value 1. Both gates are called **square-root-of-NOT** gates. They both pass the target line value through unaltered if the control has value 0.*

Definition 4. *A **controlled-controlled-V** gate is the extension of the controlled-V gate to the case of two controls both of which must be 1 to apply the transformation to the target. A **controlled-controlled-V$^+$** gate is the analogous extension to the controlled-V$^+$ gate.*

Let $\mathbf{W} = \mathbf{R}_4 = \frac{1}{2} \begin{pmatrix} 1+\sqrt{i} & 1-\sqrt{i} \\ 1-\sqrt{i} & 1+\sqrt{i} \end{pmatrix}$. Its adjoint is $\mathbf{W}^+ = \frac{1}{2} \begin{pmatrix} 1-i\sqrt{i} & 1+i\sqrt{i} \\ 1+i\sqrt{i} & 1-i\sqrt{i} \end{pmatrix}$. By definition, $\mathbf{W} \times \mathbf{W} = \mathbf{V}$. It follows directly that $\mathbf{W}^+ \times \mathbf{W}^+ = \mathbf{V}^+$. It is readily verified that $\mathbf{W}^+ = \mathbf{W}^{-1}$.

Definition 5. *A **controlled-W** gate applies the transformation defined by the matrix $\mathbf{W}$ when the single control line has value 1. Likewise, a **controlled-W$^+$** gate applies the transformation defined by the matrix $\mathbf{W}^+$ when the single control line has value 1. Both gates are called **fourth-root-of-NOT** gates.*

The quantum bit operations corresponding to the matrices V, V^+, W and W^+ are rotations around the x-axis of the Bloch sphere [5]. V and W define rotations by 90° and 45° in one direction while V^+ and W^+ define rotations by 90° and 45° in the opposite direction. Considering computation, we note from the well-known De Moivre's theorem that $i^{1/k} = \cos\frac{\pi}{2k} + i\sin\frac{\pi}{2k}$. Hence $\sqrt{i} = \cos\frac{\pi}{4} + i\sin\frac{\pi}{4}$.

The above can be extended to gates implementing other roots-of-NOT. Higher order roots require progressively smaller rotation angles. We do not consider that option here and, for that reason, we do not consider the case of two-control W and W^+ gates.

The following properties and definitions are useful for simplifying circuits.

Property 1. MCT gates, including NOT, CNOT and Toffoli gates, are self-inverse and two identical such gates in a row yield the identity mapping. V and V^+ gates with the same target and the same control are the inverse of each other. W and W^+ gates with the same target and the same control are the inverse of each other.

Property 2. Given a cascade of gates $G_1 G_2 \ldots G_k$ realizing the reversible function F, the cascade $G_k^{-1} \ldots G_2^{-1} G_1^{-1}$ realizes the function F^{-1}, where G_i^{-1} is the inverse gate for G_i.

Definition 6. *Since an MCT gate is self-inverse applying Property 2 to a realization of the gate yields an alternate realization for the same gate. We term this the* **reverse** *realization.*

Property 3. In a circuit realizing a reversible function, the functionality is not changed if for any line, (a) all V gates are replaced by V^+ gates and all V^+ gates are replaced by V gates, or (b) all W gates are replaced by W^+ gates and all W^+ gates are replaced by W gates, where both interchanges must be applied to any line that contains both V-type and W-type gates.

Property 3 is the observation that we can reverse the direction of rotation in the Bloch sphere so long as we do it consistently.

The methods discussed below produce circuits composed of NOT, $CNOT$, and controlled-V, V^+, W and W^+ gates. We term such circuits NCVW circuits. We compare our results to NCV circuits which are similar except they contain no controlled-W or controlled-W^+ gates.

Definition 7. *The* **cost** *of an NCVW or NCV circuit is taken to be the number of gates, i.e. we assume NOT, CNOT and single control quantum gates all have cost 1.*

For drawing circuits, we follow the normal conventions of using a $\oplus$ for an MCT gate or a box containing the gate name to indicate the operation performed on the target line, and a $\bullet$ to indicate each control connection.

3   NCVW Circuits for MCT Gates

It is well known [1] that the Toffoli gate $T(\{c,b\};a)$ can be realized using 5 NCV gates as shown in Figure 1(a). This extends to realizing controlled-controlled-V

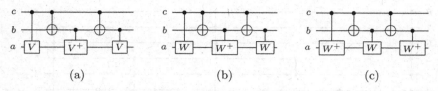

Fig. 1. (a) NCV realization of $T(\{c, b\}; a)$. (b) NCW realization of $V(\{c, b\}; a)$. (c) NCW realization of $V^+(\{c, b\}; a)$.

and V^+ gates using NCW gates as shown in Figure 1(b) and (c), respectively. Note that the circuit in Figure 1(a) represents 4 distinct realizations since it can be reversed and V and V^+ can be interchanged. The circuits in Figure 1(b) and (c) each represent two realizations by reversal.

Consider realizing $T(\{d, c, b\}; a)$. The circuit in Figure 2(a) is found by adding line d to the circuit in Figure 1(a). The correct operation of this circuit is readily verified by considering the cases of $d = 0$ and $d = 1$ in turn.

The circuit in Figure 2(b) is derived from 2(a) by (i) substituting an instance of the circuit in Figure 1(b) for the $V(\{d, c\}; a)$ gate, (ii) substituting a reversed instance of the circuit in Figure 1(c) for the $V^+(\{d, b\}; a)$ gate, and (iii) substituting an instance of the circuit in Figure 1(b) for the $V(\{d, b\}; a)$ gate. Note that once substituted two gates from (ii) cancel with two gates from (iii). Hence the gates $V^+(\{d, b\}; a)$ and $V(\{d, b\}; a)$ map to 3 gates each in the reduced circuit. The circuit in Figure 2(b) is the circuit given by Barenco et al. [1]. The construction shown here is quite different.

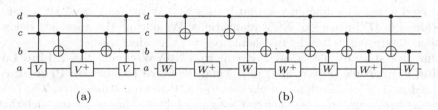

Fig. 2. (a) NCV realization of $T(\{d, c, b\}; a)$. (b) NCW circuit for $T(\{d, c, b\}; a)$.

In [7], we have shown how to decompose an MCT gate into a circuit composed of controlled-W, controlled-W^+ and MCT gates with fewer controls. An example for 7 controls and 1 ancillary line (labeled 1) is shown in Figure 3. Using the general form of this decomposition and using the circuits in Figures 1(b), 1(c) and 2(b) it is possible to build a catalog of MCT realizations for any number of controls. Further, separate circuits can be derived for differing numbers of available ancillary lines. See [7] for details.

Table 1(a) shows the costs of the NCVW realizations of MCT gates for up to 20 controls. Note that no NCVW realizations exist for 0 ancillary lines and greater than 3 controls. A blank entry at the right end of a row means the cost

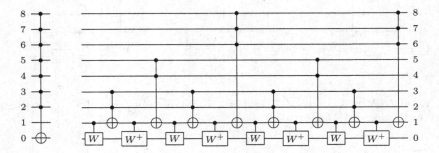

Fig. 3. Example Decomposition of a 7-control MCT Gate

can not be reduced by adding another ancillary line. For comparison, Table 1(b) shows the costs of NCV realizations of MCT gates as presented in [4]. Note that the NCVW are consistently cheaper and for 3 controls and 7 or more controls one less ancillary line is required to achieve the smallest circuit.

4   NCVW Circuits for MCT Circuits

The previous section addressed finding an NCVW realization for a single MCT gate and how that can be used to build a catalog of NCVW realizations for individual MCT gates with particular numbers of controls and ancillary lines. Here, we consider how such a catalog can be used in transforming a MCT gate circuit to an NCVW circuit. The approach described here is similar to the one presented in [8]. The difference is that it uses NCVW realizations of MCT gates developed in [7] in place of NCV realizations. We outline the approach below. Readers interested in full details should consult the references.

Our procedure to map a MCT circuit to a NCVW circuit uses a **Line Labeling Procedure** (Procedure 1 of [8]) and the **Gate Reduction Procedure** (Procedure 2 of [8]). Both are applicable to MCT and quantum gates. The Line Labeling Procedure traverses a circuit assigning labels to line segments such that two segments on the same line that are assigned the same label have identical functionality. This is done by identifying gate sequences that realize the identity function using a stack of gates for each circuit line. The Gate Reduction Procedure finds possible cancelations and reductions in the circuit by moving gates across the circuit and making them adjacent to every gate in their movement domain. It starts from one end of the circuit and labels one gate at a time. Then it moves that gate back through the circuit as far as possible to find the best reduction. The gate either may be canceled with its inverse or may be reduced to a single gate when combined with other gates.

The key extension to the Gate Reduction Procedure as given in [8] to incorporate W and W^+ gates, was to modify the gate combining step so that it considers more than two gates at a time to find possible reductions. As a gate (G_p) is moved across the circuit, a list is made that contains gates that can be

Table 1. Cost of MCT gate circuits: (a) NCVW cost, (b) NCV cost

Controls	Number of Ancillary Lines							
	0	1	2	3	4	5	6	7
0	1							
1	1							
2	5							
3	13							
4		20						
5		28						
6		40						
7		52						
8		64						
9		80	76					
10		96	88					
11		112	104	100				
12		128	120	112				
13		152	136	128	124			
14		176	158	144	136			
15		200	176	160	152	148		
16		224	200	176	168	160		
17		248	224	200	184	176	172	
18		272	248	224	200	192	184	
19		296	272	248	224	208	200	196
20		320	296	272	248	224	216	208

(a)

Controls	Number of Ancillary Lines								
	0	1	2	3	4	5	6	7	8
0	1								
1	1								
2	5								
3		14							
4		20							
5		32							
6		44							
7		64	56						
8		76	68						
9		96	88	80					
10		108	100	92					
11		132	120	112	104				
12		156	132	124	116				
13		180	156	148	136	128			
14		204	180	172	148	140			
15		228	204	198	172	160	152		
16		252	228	222	196	172	164		
17		276	252	246	222	196	184	176	
18		300	276	270	246	220	196	188	
19		324	300	294	270	246	220	208	200
20		348	324	318	294	270	244	220	212

(b)

adjacent to G_p and have the same target and control as G_p with the same labels on their controls. Then, the gates in this list are removed from the circuit and an optimized equivalent sequence is inserted in the position of the left-most removed gate in the circuit. For example a sequence of VNW^+ gates will be replaced by NW. The optimized equivalent sequence may be empty which indicates that the corresponding set of gates realizes the identity function.

The MCT to NCVW mapping procedure is similar to Procedure 4 in [8]. It first optimizes the MCT cascade using the Gate Reduction Procedure described above. Then, MCT gates are expanded to their equivalent NCVW cascades pairwise to find optimizations across gate boundaries. To achieve this, an MCT gate is made adjacent to all other MCT gates in its movement domain and the pair that introduces the most reduction when expanding to its NCVW realization is selected. In pairwise expansion, alternative NCVW realizations such as reverse realizations, $V - V^+$, and $W - W^+$ substitutions are examined to find the best reduction. At the last step of the mapping procedure, the resulting NCVW circuit is optimized using the Gate Reduction Procedure.

Figure 4 shows the results of applying the above procedures for the NCV and NCVW libraries for the REVLIB benchmark circuit decod24-v1_24. The MCT circuit from REVLIB is shown in Figure 4(a). The NCV circuit is shown in

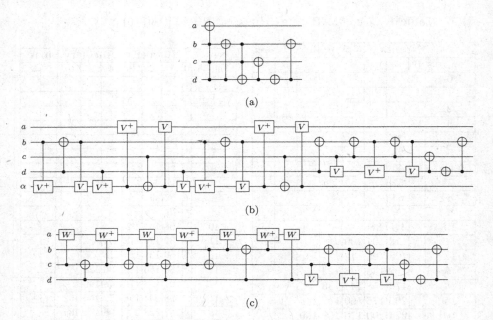

Fig. 4. Example decod24-v1_24 circuits: (a) MCT from REVLIB [9], (b) NCV, (c) NCVW

Figure 4(b) and the NCVW circuit is shown in Figure 4(c). The NCV circuit has a cost of 23 while the NCVW circuit has a cost of 20. The NCV circuit uses an added ancillary line labeled α. The NCVW does not need an ancillary line. This is because the widest gate in the MCT circuit has 3 controls and as shown in Table 1 such a gate has a 13 gate NCVW realization with no ancillary line. For a MCT circuit with more than 4 lines with a gate using all lines, an added ancillary line is required in an NCVW circuit.

The leftmost 14 gates in Figure 4(b) are an NCV realization of the $T(\{d, c, b\}; a)$ gate in 4(a). They are followed by the $T(d; b)$ gate and then by a five gate realization of the $T(b, c; d)$ in 4(a). Lastly, the final three gates in 4(a) are copied over to 4(b).

Figure 4(c) is constructed in a similar way. The first 12 gates are from the 13 gate NCVW realization of $T(a, b, c; d)$. The 13th gate does not appear as it is $T(d; b)$ and cancels with the existing occurrence of that gate in Figure 4(a). The final 8 gates in Figure 4(c) are the same as in Figure 4(b).

5   Experimental Results

We have implemented the methods described above using Python 2.6.5. The circuits considered are from the REVLIB web site [9]. Our experiments were run on a system with a 3.2 GHz i5-650 CPU and 3.0 GB RAM.

Table 2. NCVW realizations of selected REVLIB benchmarks

REVLIB Circuit	REVLIB Cost	Initial Cost	MCT Gate Reduction	Quantum Gate Substitution	Quantum Gate Reduction	% Cost Reduction	CPU (sec.)
sym9_148	4368	3612	665	665	659	84.91	25.906
sym6_145	777	543	203	201	199	74.39	4.719
plus63mod8192_164*	45025	22208	19318	18863	18856	58.12	109.157
plus63mod4096_163*	32539	16808	14322	13820	13813	57.55	81.984
plus127mod8192_162*	73357	41002	35550	34193	34178	53.41	218.672
rd32-v0_66	12	12	12	8	6	50.00	0.047
rd32-v1_68	13	13	13	9	7	46.15	0.078
4gt4-v0_73*	89	80	48	48	48	46.07	0.485
rd53_133	128	104	86	78	72	43.75	0.937
cycle10_2_110	1202	694	694	682	682	43.26	3.250
hwb8_114*	14699	9131	8888	8392	8378	43.00	142.516
hwb8_115*	14691	9131	8888	8392	8378	42.97	142.906
hwb8_113*	16530	10736	10282	9804	9787	40.79	78.500
hwb8_118*	16522	10736	10282	9804	9787	40.76	78.469
hwb9_123*	22510	13494	13492	13456	13434	40.32	185.672
rd53_134	120	104	86	78	72	40.00	0.922
ham15_107	1831	1509	1184	1115	1107	39.54	14.188
hwb9_119*	44714	29842	29010	27389	27340	38.86	272.609
hwb9_121*	44665	29805	28982	27359	27311	38.85	258.141
hwb9_120*	44702	29842	29010	27389	27340	38.84	260.406
hwb9_122*	44653	29805	28982	27359	27311	38.84	257.672
4gt12-v0_86*	58	49	38	36	36	37.93	0.328
4gt12-v0_87*	54	45	34	34	34	37.04	0.187
4gt4-v0_72*	54	45	34	34	34	37.04	0.281
hwb7_59*	5236	3772	3613	3363	3352	35.98	58.438
hwb8_116*	7015	4547	4547	4505	4496	35.91	108.171
hwb8_117*	7013	4547	4547	4505	4496	35.89	108.219
4mod5-v1_22	9	9	9	7	6	33.33	0.047
4mod5-v1_23	24	24	18	16	16	33.33	0.172
peres_9	6	6	6	4	4	33.33	0.015
hwb7_60*	4170	2966	2844	2838	2829	32.16	30.234
4mod5-v0_18	25	25	19	17	17	32.00	0.141
4mod5-v0_19	13	13	10	9	9	30.77	0.047
mod5mils_65	13	13	10	9	9	30.77	0.093
mod5mils_71	13	13	10	9	9	30.77	0.094
toffoli_double_4	10	10	7	7	7	30.00	0.078
hwb7_61*	3876	2974	2906	2743	2731	29.54	41.891
hwb6_57*	1171	913	845	836	833	28.86	7.671
hwb7_62*	2611	1901	1901	1884	1878	28.07	18.719
rd53_138	44	44	44	35	32	27.27	0.594
4gt12-v0_88*	41	32	32	30	30	26.83	0.172
hwb6_56*	1530	1227	1204	1126	1122	26.67	17.656
rd32-v0_67	8	12	12	8	6	25.00	0.047
rd53_135	77	71	68	59	58	24.68	1.313
hwb4_49*	65	65	57	51	49	24.62	0.438
rd53_131	119	101	95	91	90	24.37	1.125
4gt4-v0_80*	37	28	28	28	28	24.32	0.172
rd73_140	76	76	76	61	58	23.68	1.016
sys6-v0_111	72	72	72	59	55	23.61	1.141
rd53_132	117	101	95	91	90	23.08	1.125
alu-v2_31	101	101	84	78	78	22.77	0.578
rd53_136	75	71	68	59	58	22.67	1.297
4gt4-v0_79*	49	40	40	38	38	22.45	0.375
4mod5-v0_20	9	9	9	7	7	22.22	0.047
decod24-v0_38	18	18	18	14	14	22.22	0.047
decod24-v2_43	18	18	18	14	14	22.22	0.079
ham3_102	9	9	9	7	7	22.22	0.031
hwb4_50*	63	65	57	51	49	22.22	0.437
rd32-v1_69	9	13	13	9	7	22.22	0.062
3_17_13	14	14	14	11	11	21.43	0.125
4gt4-v0_78*	53	44	44	44	42	20.75	0.265
ham15_108	453	387	378	362	360	20.53	5.485
4gt12-v1_89*	45	36	36	36	36	20.00	0.156
fredkin_6	15	15	15	13	12	20.00	0.031
ham3_103	10	10	10	8	8	20.00	0.047
rd84_142	112	112	112	94	90	19.64	2.640
sym9_146	108	108	108	88	87	19.44	1.422
mod5d2_70	16	16	13	13	13	18.75	0.109
4mod7-v0_94	38	38	38	32	31	18.42	0.125
4mod7-v0_95	38	38	38	32	31	18.42	0.125
mod5adder_127	125	107	107	104	102	18.40	1.266
mod5d1_63	11	11	11	10	9	18.18	0.078
4mod7-v1_96	39	39	39	33	32	17.95	0.188
rd53_130	232	196	196	192	191	17.67	2.579
4gt4-v1_74*	57	48	48	47	47	17.54	0.218
4_49_16*	60	60	57	53	50	16.67	0.406
4gt13_91*	30	30	27	25	25	16.67	0.157
one-two-three-v0_98	40	40	40	34	34	15.00	0.187
	458551	284605	264825	253107	252662	44.90	2555.423

Table 3. Benchmarks for which the NCVW cost is greater than the NCV cost

REVLIB Circuit	NCV Cost [8]	NCVW Cost	% Cost Increase
4gt4-v1_74*	46	47	-2.17
ham15_108	356	360	-1.12
one-two-three-v0_97	62	63	-1.61
one-two-three-v1_99	31	32	-3.23

Table 2 presents the results for a number of benchmark circuits from REVLIB. Our program applies the methods above to the circuit in both the forward and the reverse direction. A * after the circuit name indicates the addition of a single ancillary line because the circuit contains at least one MCT gate that uses all lines in the circuit.

The results are reported for each circuit for the better of the two directions. We report (1) the quantum cost from REVLIB, (2) the initial NCVW cost which is found by replacing MCT gates by the NCVW catalog circuits corresponding to Table 1, (3) the NCVW costs after MCT gate reduction is applied, (4) the NCVW cost after quantum gate expansion, (5) the NCVW cost after quantum gate reduction which is the NCVW cost of the final circuit, (6) the percentage cost reduction comparing the final NCVW cost to the REVLIB cost and (7) the CPU time for all steps. Overall, our methods yield a 44.9% improvement compared to the costs reported in REVLIB. The majority of the improvement (37.9%) comes from the catalog circuits. The rest comes from our quantum expansion and quantum reduction techniques.

Table 3 shows the four cases where the NCVW circuit is more costly than the NCV circuit. This results from the fact that our methods use many heuristics.

Table 4 shows the benchmarks for which the NCVW circuit is an improvement over the NCV circuit. The overall improvement for these examples is 4.71%.

As noted, our method adds an extra ancillary line if the MCT circuit includes a gate that uses all circuit lines. This is not the case for the results reported in REVLIB. However, the cost model employed in REVLIB is based on the work in Barenco et al. [1] which assumes a 2^{c-1}-th root-of-NOT gate is available to realize a c-control MCT gate in a circuit with $c + 1$ lines. We anticipate that realizing gates progressively higher roots of NOT may be prohibitive in many technologies and adding one extra line will be preferable. Also we expect that synthesis methods can be made to avoid the situation in most cases.

6   Conclusions and Future Work

The benchmark results presented show that the methods described in this paper can lead to notably smaller quantum circuits than reported in REVLIB and other work. The results also show that using W and W^+ gates leads to smaller circuits than those using NCV gates. We thus conclude that the approach taken is quite promising and should be further refined.

Table 4. Benchmarks where NCVW circuit cost is less than NCV circuit cost

REVLIB Circuit	NCV Cost [8]	NCVW Cost	% Cost Reduction
4_49_16*	55	50	9.09
4gt10-v1_81	35	32	8.57
4gt12-v1_89*	37	36	2.7
4gt13_91	28	25	10.7
4gt4-v0_73*	49	48	2.04
4gt4-v0_78*	45	42	6.67
4gt4-v0_79*	41	38	7.32
4gt5_75	22	21	4.55
4gt5_76	27	26	3.7
4gt5_77	28	26	7.14
4mod7-v0_94	32	31	3.13
4mod7-v0_95	32	31	3.13
4mod7-v1_96	33	32	3.03
alu-v2_30*	103	98	4.85
alu-v2_31	83	78	6.02
alu-v2_32	38	35	7.89
alu-v4_36	28	27	3.57
cycle10_2_110	720	682	5.28
decod24-enable_126	77	75	2.6
decod24-v1_41*	23	20	13
decod24-v3_45*	35	31	11.4
ham15_107	1155	1107	4.16
ham15_109	198	190	4.04
ham7_104	84	76	9.52
ham7_105	64	59	7.81
hwb4_49*	54	49	9.26
hwb4_50*	54	49	9.26
hwb4_51*	73	71	2.74
hwb5_53*	282	270	4.26
hwb5_54*	234	220	5.98
hwb5_55	95	93	2.11
hwb6_56*	1150	1122	2.43
hwb6_57*	872	833	4.47
hwb6_58	132	127	3.79
hwb7_59*	3500	3352	4.23
hwb7_60*	2989	2829	5.35
hwb7_61*	2863	2731	4.61
hwb7_62*	1973	1878	4.82
hwb8_113*	10328	9787	5.24
hwb8_114*	8815	8378	4.96
hwb8_115*	8815	8378	4.96
hwb8_116*	4825	4496	6.82
hwb8_117*	4825	4496	6.82
hwb8_118*	10328	9787	5.24
hwb9_119*	28660	27340	4.61
hwb9_120*	28660	27340	4.61
hwb9_121*	28629	27311	4.6
hwb9_122*	28629	27311	4.6
hwb9_123*	14487	13434	7.27
mod5adder_127	104	102	1.92
mod5adder_128	84	80	4.76
mod5adder_129	76	74	2.63
one-two-three-v0_98	35	34	2.86
plus127mod8192_162*	35348	34178	3.31
plus63mod4096_163*	14652	13813	5.73
plus63mod8192_164*	19566	18856	3.63
rd53_130	195	191	2.05
rd53_135	59	58	1.69
rd53_136	59	58	1.69
rd53_137	59	58	1.69
sym6_145	212	199	6.13
sym9_148	672	659	1.93
Total	**265465**	**252958**	**4.71**

Our future work in this area will include extending the work to handle negative controls for MCT gates (controls that are activated by the value 0 and not 1). Other quantum gate libraries will be considered. We will also examine how various aspects of our methods and certain heuristics in particular might be' changed to optimize the circuits even further. Lastly, except for the case of two controls, our procedure does not consider the permutation of MCT gate controls with a view to identifying more quantum gate reductions across MCT gate boundaries. We are considering how to address this. Exhaustive search is prohibitive and we have yet to determine how to identify which subset of the possible orderings will be most effective.

As noted above, two points on a line in a circuit which are assigned the same label by the line labeling procedure have the same functionality. The converse is not true, i.e. two points with the same functionality may be assigned different labels. As a result, our methods can miss certain reductions. We are investigating replacing the line labels with decision diagrams that will guarantee finding all functional equivalences. It remain to be seen whether the advantage gained will justify the added complexity and computational time.

References

1. Barenco, A., Bennett, C., Cleve, R., DiVincenzo, D., Margolus, M., Shor, P., Sleator, T., Smolin, J., Weinfurter, H.: Elementary gates for quantum computation. Physical Review A 52(5), 3457–3467 (1995)
2. Fredkin, E., Toffoli, T.: Conservative logic. Int'l J. of Theoretical Physics 21, 219–253 (1982)
3. Miller, D.M., Wille, R., Dueck, G.W.: Synthesizing reversible circuits from irreversible specifications using Reed-Muller spectral techniques. In: Proc. Reed-Muller Workshop, pp. 87–96 (May 2009)
4. Miller, D.M., Wille, R., Sasanian, Z.: Elementary quantum gate realizations for multiple-control Toffolli gates. In: Proc. Int'l Symp. on Multiple-valued Logic, pp. 288–293 (2011)
5. Nielsen, M., Chuang, I.: Quantum Computation and Quantum Information. Cambridge Univ. Press (2000)
6. Peres, A.: Reversible logic and quantum computers. Physical Review A 32, 3266–3276 (1985)
7. Sasanian, Z., Miller, D.M.: NCVW quantum gate realization of mixed control MCT gates. IEEE Trans. on CAD (2011) (submitted)
8. Sasanian, Z., Miller, D.M.: A new methodology for optimizing quantum realizations of reversible circuits. ACM J. on Emerging Technologies in Computing Systems (2011) (submitted)
9. Wille, R., Große, D., Teuber, L., Dueck, G.W., Drechsler, R.: RevLib: An online resource for reversible functions and reversible circuits. In: Int'l Symp. on Multi-Valued Logic, pp. 220–225 (2008), RevLib, www.revlib.org
10. Wille, R., Drechsler, R.: Synthesis of Boolean Functions in Reversible Logic. In: Progress in Applications of Boolean Functions (Synthesis Lectures on Digital Circuits and Systems). Morgan and Claypool (2010)
11. Wille, R., Große, D., Miller, D.M., Drechsler, R.: Equivalence checking of reversible circuits. In: Proc. Int'l Symp. on Multiple-valued Logic (CD), 7p (2009)

Changing the Gate Order for Optimal LNN Conversion

Atsushi Matsuo and Shigeru Yamashita

Graduate School of Science and Engineering Ritsumeikan University
1-1-1 Noji Higashi, Kusatsu, Shiga 525-8577, Japan
comp@ngc.is.ritsumei.ac.jp, ger@cs.ritsumei.ac.jp

Abstract. While several physical realization schemes have been proposed for future quantum information processing, most known facts suggest that quantum information processing should have intrinsic limitations; physically realizable operations would be only interaction between neighbor qubits. To use only such physically realizable operations, we need to convert a general quantum circuit into one for an so-called Linear Nearest Neighbor (LNN) architecture where any gates should be operated between only adjacent qubits. Thus, there has been much attention to develop efficient methods to design quantum circuits for an LNN architecture. Most of the existing researches do not consider changing the gate order of the original circuit, and thus the result may not be optimal. In this paper, we propose a method to convert a quantum circuit into one for an LNN architecture with the smallest number of SWAP gates. Our method improves the previous result for Approximate Quantum Fourier Transform (AQFT) by the state-of-the-art design method.

Keywords: Quantum Circuit, Linear Nearest Neighbor, Adjacent Transposition Graph.

1 Introduction

Since the invention of the integrated circuit in 1958, the number of transistors on an integrated circuit has doubled approximately every two years. Moreover, the size of transistors has been decreased by the advance of the semiconductor technology. However the size of transistors cannot be smaller than the atomic scale: we are approaching to the fundamental limits of the advance of the semiconductor technology.

Consequently, much attention has been paid to another computing paradigm such as quantum computing [1]. A quantum computer is a device to make computations by exploiting quantum mechanical phenomena, which enables to solve some problems more efficiently than classical computers such as factoring of numbers [2].

Several impressive researches have been studied for physically implementing quantum computers. With the advance of the quantum computing technology, it is getting clearer that there should be some intrinsic limitations on implementing quantum computers [3]. One of such limitations is that we cannot interact apart qubits by one basic operation [4]. By this intrinsic limitation, it is considered very difficult to make an interaction between two far apart qubits for most quantum technologies. For this reason, quantum circuits may be realized on an so-called Linear Nearest Neighbor (LNN) architecture which permits interactions only between adjacent (nearest neighbor) qubits.

A. De Vos and R. Wille (Eds.): RC 2011, LNCS 7165, pp. 89–101, 2012.

Therefore, for the coming "quantum computing era," it should be very important to establish a design technology for quantum circuits on an LNN architecture. Indeed, there have been many researches for this issue. Some researches designed specific quantum circuits on an LNN architecture manually, e. g., circuits for approximate quantum Fourier transform [5], Shor's factorization algorithm [4,6], quantum addition [7], and quantum error correction [8]. Others have developed methods to design general quantum circuits on an LNN architecture. For example, Hirata et al. proposed a heuristic to convert any quantum circuits to one for an LNN architecture [9]. Their method inserts SWAP gates in an initial circuit so that all gates are performed on adjacent qubits. Recently, Saeedi et al. have developed a very efficient design framework that utilizes their ideas of template matching and reordering strategies. The LNN AQFT circuit designed manually [5] has been improved by [9], and then successively improved further by [10]. Most of the above-mentioned techniques adopt the insertion of SWAP gates and the reorder of the initial qubit lines. In their methods, it has not been considered to change the gate order of the given initial circuit.

Our Contribution. In this paper, we explicitly consider a possibility to change the initial gate order in a case where the gate reordering is possible. More precisely, we consider a problem to find the smallest number of added SWAP gates for the LNN conversion by changing the order of gates if they can commute. Our main contribution is to formulate such a problem as a search problem on the *adjacent transposition graph*. Accordingly we can find the best solution with respect to the number of SWAP gates to be added. Our method can find an AQFT circuit with the fewest SWAP gates, which improved the result by [10].

The remainder of this paper is organized as follows. In Section 2, quantum circuits and LNN architectures are explained. Section 3 describes the adjacent transposition graph and our proposed method. We then provide experimental results in Section 4. Finally, we conclude this paper with a summary and future works in Section 5.

2   Preliminaries

In this section, we provide some basics necessary for our paper.

2.1   Quantum Circuit

A quantum circuit is a model of quantum computing. A quantum circuit indicates the order of basic unitary operators (called quantum gates) corresponding to a given quantum algorithm. Quantum bits and quantum gates are drawn on quantum circuits. An example of a quantum circuit is shown in Fig. 1, where each horizontal line indicates a quantum bit (denoted by "Qubit 1" to "Qubit 5"), and each dashed circle indicate a specific unitary operation called a quantum gate. On quantum circuits, time flows from left to right which means that quantum gates are applied from the leftmost gate in sequence. We explain quantum bits and quantum gates in detail below.

Quantum Bit. While in classical computers, a bit has to be either 1 or 0, in quantum computer, quantum bits (qubits in short) can be 1, 0 or the superposition state as $|\psi\rangle = \alpha|0\rangle + \beta|1\rangle$ which is the any linear combination of 1 and 0.

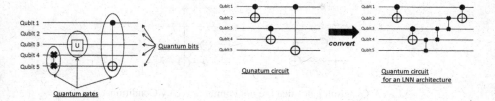

Fig. 1. A quantum circuit

Fig. 2. Conversion of a quantum circuit to an LNN circuit

Quantum Gate. A quantum circuit consists of a cascade of quantum gates. A quantum gate indicates what unitary operator is applied to which qubit. For example, in Fig. 1, the leftmost gate indicates that a SWAP gate is applied to Qubits 4 and 5. The following three gates are mainly used in this paper.

- A SWAP gate is the leftmost gate in Fig. 1. A SWAP gate has two target bits x_{t1} and x_{t2}, and interchanges the values of the target bits.
- A one-qubit unitary gate is the middle gate in Fig. 1. A one-qubit unitary gate applies any unitary operations to the target bit.
- A CNOT gate is the rightmost gate in Fig. 1. A CNOT gate has a control bit and a target bit. In Fig. 1, a control bit of the CNOT gate is Qubit 1 and a target bit of the CNOT gate is Qubit 5. The following matrices: $\sigma_x = \begin{pmatrix} 0 & 1 \\ 1 & 0 \end{pmatrix}$ is applied to its target bit iff the state of its control bit is $|1\rangle$.

CNOT gates and one-qubit gates are universal so any quantum gates can be decomposed into a combination of CNOT gates and one-qubit gates.[1]

2.2 LNN Architecture

With the advance of the quantum computing technology, it is getting clearer that there should be some intrinsic limitations on implementing quantum computers. One of such limitations is that we cannot interact apart qubits by one basic operation. By this intrinsic limitation, it is considered very difficult to make an interaction between two far apart qubits for most quantum technologies. For this reason, quantum circuits may be realized on an so-called Linear Nearest Neighbor (LNN) architecture which permits interactions only between adjacent (nearest neighbor) qubits.

If a gate interacts two far apart qubits, we can make the gate interact two adjacent qubits by inserting (possibly many) SWAP gates before the gate. Thus by inserting SWAP gates, it is possible to convert a circuit to one with the same functionality for an LNN architecture. Fig. 2 shows an example of converting a quantum circuit to one for an LNN architecture. On the left circuit of Fig. 2, two target bits of the rightmost gate are apart. By inserting SWAP gates, the quantum circuit is converted to one for an LNN architecture. The right circuit in Fig. 2 has the same functionality, and it uses interactions between only adjacent qubits. Hereafter, let **an LNN circuit** denotes a circuit for an LNN architecture, and **a non-LNN circuit** denotes a circuit for a non-LNN architecture.

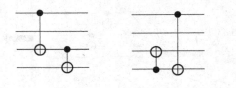

Fig. 3. Quantum gates that are not commutative by Condition 1

3   Changing the Gate Order for Optimal LNN Conversion

3.1   Problem Definition

The problem to convert a circuit into an LNN circuit is formulated as follow.

LNNizing problem. Given a quantum circuit that consists of one-qubit gates and two-qubit gates and the order of initial qubits, the problem is to convert the given quantum circuit to an LNN circuit with the smallest number of SWAP gates. The order of qubits after conversion should be the same as the initial qubits since the circuit may be used as a sub-circuit for a large quantum circuit. Formally, the input and the output of the problem are as follows.

Input : a given quantum circuit, and initial qubit order.
Output : an LNN circuit with the same qubit order as the initial one.

3.2   Dependence between Quantum Gates

In a quantum circuit, there is usually dependence between a pair of two gates such that one gate should be applied before the other gate, i. e., some gates cannot commute. When we convert a quantum circuit to an LNN circuit, the dependence between quantum gates has to be kept, otherwise the logical functionality of the quantum circuit is changed after converting it to an LNN circuit.

Quantum gates that satisfy one of the following conditions are not commutative. In the following two conditions, let two gates be A and B. Let also the control bits and the target bits of A be A_{cb} and A_{tb}, respectively. Also B_{cb} and B_{tb} have the same meaning for the gate B.

Condition 1: The first condition is that $A_{cb} = B_{tb}$. This means that the control bit of one gate is the same as the target bit of the other gate. Fig. 3 shows an example of two quantum gates that are not commutative by Condition 1.

Condition 2: The second condition is $A_{tb} = B_{tb}$ and two unitary matrices that are applied to A_{tb} and B_{tb} are not commutative. The target bits of two quantum gates are the same and the unitary matrices that are applied to the target bits are not commutative, then the two gates are not commutative. Fig. 4 shows an example of two quantum gates that are not commutative by Condition 2. The gate denoted by H (in Fig. 4) is called *Hadmard* gate that apply the following matrix: $H = \frac{1}{\sqrt{2}}\begin{pmatrix} 1 & 1 \\ 1 & -1 \end{pmatrix}$ to its target bit. The matrices σ_x and H are not commutative so that interchanging these two gates will change the logical functionality of the quantum circuit.

Fig. 4. Quantum gates that are not commutative by Condition 2

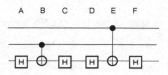

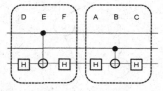

Fig. 5. Groups of quantum gates that are commutative

Fig. 6. The interchanged groups of quantum gates

A pair of quantum gates that satisfies one of the above two conditions is not commutative. If a quantum circuit has such a pair, we should not change the order of the pair of gates when we convert the circuit to an LNN circuit.

Two quantum gates cannot be interchanged (with each other) if one of the above two conditions do hold. Even in such a case, we may swap two groups of quantum gates. We do not consider such a special case in this paper, but only mention such an example below. For example, a quantum gate E and a quantum gate D or C in Fig. 5 are not commutative by Condition 2. Two quantum gates C and B in Fig. 5 are not commutative by Condition 2. Accordingly, we conclude that the two gates, E and B, cannot be swapped, and thus when we convert the circuit of Fig. 5 to an LNN circuit, we only consider the case where the gate B should be applied before gate E. However, we can swap two groups of gates in this example. Namely, the circuit in Fig. 5 can be transformed to one in Fig. 6, and thus we can also consider the case where the gate E is applied first when we convert the circuit to an LNN circuit.

In Fig. 6, despite the fact that quantum gates A, B, C and D, E, F are not commutative by Condition 2, the groups of quantum gates are commutative because interchanging two groups of the quantum gates will not change the logical functionality of the quantum circuit.

The above example tells us that we may change the order of application of two quantum gates even if either one of the two conditions holds. Considering such a possibility may reduce the cost of conversion. However it is difficult and almost impractical to consider a possibility of swapping two groups of gates; we consider only the possibility of swapping individual gates in this paper.

3.3   Gate Dependence Graph

From a non-LNN circuit, we can construct a *gate dependence graph* by considering Condition 1 and 2. A gate dependence graph is a directed graph that shows the dependence of quantum gates in a given quantum circuit. Each node, n_i, in a gate dependence graph corresponds to one specific gate, g_i, in the given circuit. An edge between two nodes n_i and n_j means that gate g_i should be applied before gate g_j, i. e., we cannot

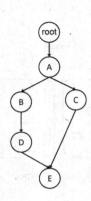

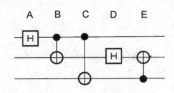

Fig. 8. A quantum circuit before LNN conversion

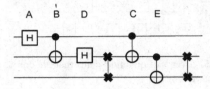

Fig. 7. A gate dependence graph

Fig. 9. A quantum circuit after LNN conversion

change the order of application of gates g_i and g_j. This can be obviously determined by Condition 1 and 2. By technical convenience, we have one special root node in a gate dependence graph. Each node connected to the root node indicates that the corresponding gate does not depend on any other gates, i. e., the gate can be applied first in the circuit. Fig. 7 shows the gate dependence graph for a quantum circuit in Fig. 8. Fig. 9 shows a quantum circuit after converting the circuit in Fig. 8 to an LNN circuit. By this conversion, the gate order is changed but the dependences of quantum gates remain unchanged.

In the following, we will use the following notation: for a set of gates Γ, and a gate dependence graph G (where we assume each gate g_i in Γ has the corresponding node n_i in G), $\kappa_{\Gamma, G}$ denotes a set of gates g having the following two properties: (1) g is included in Γ, and (2) there is no g' in Γ such that the corresponding node of g' is a predecessor of the corresponding node of g in G.

3.4   Adjacent Transposition Graph

In this section, adjacent transposition graphs are explained. In an adjacent transposition graph, a node corresponds to a permutation, and an edge corresponds to a SWAP gate. The numbers in each node indicates the order of quantum bits. Hereafter, let n denote the number of qubits of a given quantum circuit. Each node has $(n-1)$ edges. The total numbers of the nodes and the edges in an adjacent transposition graph for an n-qubit circuit are $n!$ and $\frac{(n-1)n!}{2}$, respectively. Fig. 10 is an example of an adjacent transposition graph with $n = 4$.

By finding the shortest path (in an adjacent transposition graph) corresponding to a sequence of qubit orders that realizes all quantum gates on an LNN architecture, optimal conversion that considers the order of the quantum gates is possible. In the following example, a quantum circuit in Fig. 11 is converted to an LNN circuit by utilizing an adjacent transposition graph. Fig. 12 is a gate dependence graph of the quantum circuit in Fig. 11, and Fig. 13 shows how to convert a quantum circuit to an LNN circuit by

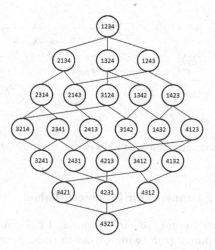

Fig. 10. A adjacent transposition graph with $n = 4$

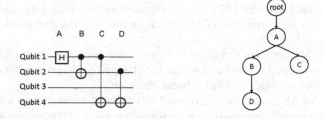

Fig. 11. A non-LNN circuit   **Fig. 12.** The gate dependence graph for the quantum circuit in Fig. 11

utilizing an adjacent transposition graph. Numbers on the quantum circuit of Fig. 13 indicates the order of the qubits at the indicated point of time.

We will use the following notations:

- A gate is said to be **LNN-realizable on the qubit order N** if it can be applied by interacting only adjacent qubits when the qubit order is N. In the following, let λ_N be a set of LNN-realizable gates on the qubit order N.

- A gate is said to be **applicable with respect to a set of gates Γ, and gate dependence graph G** (where we assume each gate g_i in Γ has the corresponding node n_i in G), if it is included in $\kappa_{\Gamma,\,G}$ defined in Sec. 3. 3.

- A gate is said to be **realizable at a qubit order N with a remaining gate set Γ and a gate dependence graph G**, if it is included in $\lambda_N \cap \kappa_{\Gamma,G}$. In other words, if the current situation permits to apply some of the gates in Γ, such gates are called "realizable". We will use this terminology in the rest of this paper.

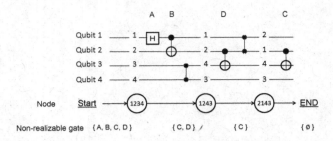

Fig. 13. Conversion of a quantum circuit to an LNN circuit by utilizing the adjacent transposition graph

3.5   Overview and an Example of the Proposed Method

Our main idea to convert a non-LNN circuit into an LNN-circuit is to formulate the problem as finding an optimal path (with respect to some desired property explained below) on an adjacent transposition graph. The overview is as follows.

We first let Γ be the set of all the gates in the given non-LNN circuit. Then, from Γ, we remove a gate one by one if the gate is realizable at the current situation. Realizable gates can be applied in the converted LNN circuit, so we remove all such gates from Γ, and place them at the end of the converted LNN circuit. In this way, the converted LNN circuit will grow.

If there is no realizable gates are remained in Γ, we insert (possibly many) SWAP gates at the end of the converted LNN circuit so that the changed qubit order make some gates in Γ realizable. We continue this until Γ becomes empty.

Note that putting a SWAP gate at the end of the LNN circuit corresponds to a move from one node to adjacent node in its adjacent transposition graph. Thus, our problem is essentially to find "the best" path in the adjacent transposition graph.

Now let us provide with an example to help understanding the above. The quantum circuit in Fig. 11 is composed of four gates A, B, C and D. At first, we set $\Gamma = \{A, B, C, D\}$.

The initial qubit order is $N = 1234$, and $\lambda_{1234} = \{A, B\}$. In Fig. 12, $\kappa_{\Gamma, G} = \{A\}$ at first. Then $\lambda_{1234} \cap \kappa_{\Gamma, G} = \{A\}$, and thus A can be applied in an LNN circuit. After placing A at the LNN circuit, we remove A from Γ. This can be formally written as $\Gamma \leftarrow \Gamma \setminus \lambda_{1234} \cap \kappa_{\Gamma, G}$. By removing A from Γ, Γ will be changed and so does $\kappa_{\Gamma, G}$. The new $\kappa_{\Gamma, G}$ will be $\kappa_{\Gamma, G} = \{B, C\}$. Therefore new realizable quantum gates will be $\lambda_{1234} \cap \kappa_{\Gamma, G} = \{B\}$, and B can be applied in the LNN circuit. In Fig. 13, when $N = 1234$, quantum gates, A and B, are realized on an LNN architecture.

After realizing quantum gates, the other quantum gates sometimes become realizable like quantum gates, A and B. For this reason, the operation $\Gamma \leftarrow \Gamma \setminus \lambda_N \cap \kappa_{\Gamma, G}$ is repeated until $\lambda_N \cap \kappa_{\Gamma, G}$ becomes ϕ.

By inserting a SWAP gate, $N = 1234$ can be changed to $N = 1243$. Then $\lambda_{1243} = \{D\}$ and $\kappa_{\Gamma, G} = \{C, D\}$. Therefore $\lambda_{1243} \cap \kappa_{\Gamma, G} = \{D\}$ so we remove D from Γ. Again, this can be written as $\Gamma \leftarrow \Gamma \setminus \lambda_{1243} \cap \kappa_{\Gamma, G}$. In Fig. 13, when $N = 1243$, the quantum gate D is realized on an LNN architecture. Then the new $\kappa_{\Gamma, G}$ is $\kappa_{\Gamma, G} = \{C\}$ and $\lambda_{1243} \cap \kappa_{\Gamma, G}$ is ϕ, and so we go to the next order of the qubits.

Algorithm 1. BFS by using ATG (Γ, N, G).

```
 1:  Γ ← Γ \ λ_N ∩ κ_{Γ, G}
 2:  if Γ is φ then
 3:      terminate searching
 4:  end if
 5:  M ← φ
 6:  M[N] ← {Γ}
 7:  Q.push ( (N, Γ) )
 8:  while  Q is not empty do
 9:      (N, Γ) ← Q.pop()
10:      for all N′ ∈ the adjacent nodes of N do
11:          while  λ_{N′} ∩ κ_{Γ, G} is not φ do
12:              Γ ← Γ \ λ_{N′} ∩ κ_{Γ, G}
13:          end while
14:          if Γ is φ then
15:              terminate searching
16:          else
17:              if M[N′] has not been registered then
18:                  M[N′] ← {Γ}
19:                  Q.push ( (N′, Γ) )
20:              else
21:                  if ∃x ∈ M[N′] such that x ⊆ Γ then
22:                      continue
23:                  else
24:                      M[N′] ← M[N′] ∪ {Γ}
25:                      Q.push ( (N′, Γ) )
26:                  end if
27:              end if
28:          end if
29:      end for
30:  end while
```

By utilizing the adjacent transposition graph in Fig. 10, we can essentially do the above procedure to convert the quantum circuit in Fig. 11 to the LNN circuit in Fig. 13. In the next section, we will describe a formal algorithm to do so as the breadth first search on an adjacent transposition graph.

3.6   The Breadth First Search by Utilizing the Adjacent Transposition Graph

Now we are ready to show our breadth first search algorithm formally as *Algorithm 1*. In the algorithm, M is a map from a qubit order to a set of sets of quantum gates that have not been placed on a converted LNN circuit yet. Q is a queue of pairs of the order of qubits, and quantum gates that have not been made realizable yet. For a qubit order (which is a permutation) N, there is the corresponding node in the adjacent transposition graph, and they are conceptually the same. Therefore, for an easy writing, we will use the notation N to mean a qubit order, or a node in the adjacent transposition graph, interchangeably depending on the context.

In the breadth first search, we may get to the same permutation node many times during the breadth first search. If the search get to the same (permutation) node again and there is no essential improvement in the set of gates that have not been made realizable, it is useless to continue the further search from the node. The reason is that we can always find the better solution from the same (permutation) node that has been visited before.

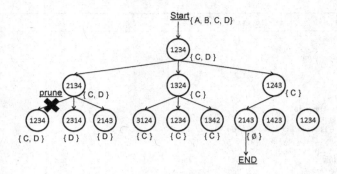

Fig. 14. The breadth first search by utilizing the adjacent transposition graph

We now explain the detail of the *Algorithm 1*. From lines 1 to 7, variables are initialized. If a given quantum circuit can be converted to an LNN circuit with no SWAP gates, we terminate the search at line 2. The breadth first search starts from line 8. At line 9, we pop a pair of a permutation N and gate set Γ from the queue, and we keep searching from the permutation node N. To do so, from line 10 to line 13, we move to the adjacent node, N', of N one by one, and we remove some gates that become realizable at the move (if any) from Γ. This operation can be formally written at lines 11 to 13.

If Γ becomes empty, we can conclude that we have found the best solution, and thus we stop the further search at line 14.

The lines after line 17 are for pruning the redundant search (from the same permutation node with no improvement from the previous visit) as mentioned above. In the algorithm, M is used as a cache to store the previous results not to perform the redundant search.

The detail is explained in the following. From lines 17 to 19, the case when $M[N']$ has not been registered indicates that the node N' in the adjacent transposition graph has never bee visited while searching. In such a case, Γ is registered into $M[N']$, and the pair of N and Γ is pushed into the queue.

The lines after line 21 deal with the case when $M[N']$ has already been registered. This indicates that the node N' in the adjacent transposition graph has already been visited while searching. In this case, we need to check whether further search from this node is useful or not. One searching path is not useful when (previous) another search path has already visited the same node N' in the adjacent transposition graph, and the set of the quantum gates that have not been made realizable yet at that time is the subset of Γ. This condition is checked at line 21.

In the example as shown in Fig 14, the left most node satisfies the above condition, and thus the further search from this node is pruned. When $N = 1234$ is visited at the first time (the starting node of the graph), the set of the quantum gates that have not been made realizable yet is $\{C, D\}$. When $N = 1234$ is visited again at the left most node, the quantum gates that have not been made realizable yet is $\{C, D\}$. Accordingly, the further search is pruned because $\{C, D\} \subseteq \{C, D\}$. This means that there is no possibility to find the better answer even if the search is continued.

Table 1. Experimental results

Circuit	n	gc	naive method # of SWAP gates	naive method Time (sec)	proposed method # of SWAP gates	proposed method Time (sec)
3_17_15	3	10	4	0.01	4	0.01
decod24-v0_40	4	9	6	0.01	6	0.01
decod24-v1_42	4	9	6	0.01	6	0.01
decod24-v2_44	4	9	6	0.01	6	0.01
decod24-v3_46	4	9	6	0.01	6	0.01
fredkin_5	3	7	2	0.01	2	0.01
miller_12	3	8	6	0.01	2	0.01
toffoli_double_3	4	7	8	0.01	4	0.01
SteaneEncoding	7	14	26	1.43	18	1.85
SteaneErrorDetection	10	12	38	1.42	34	4572.59
add8_173	25	48	46	0.33	–	–

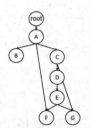

Fig. 15. The gate dependence graph of *fredkin_5*

4   Experimental Results

In this section, we show some experimental results. The proposed method was implemented in C++, and the experiments were done on an Intel Core i7-929 2.66GHz with 24GB memory.

Before showing our results, we would like to note that our method can always find the best result with respect to the number of SWAP gates. Therefore, we do not need to show the comparison with respect to the quality of the converted results. The reason is that our method essentially performs an exhaustive search. Thus, we show (1) how large problems our method can treat, and (2) how close the results of a naive method are to the best results (by our method). Also, we would like to show that (3) our method could indeed find better results compared to the state-of-the-art existing method.

To show the above (1) and (2), we compared the proposed method to the naive approach, in which the gate order is not considered, i. e., the gate order is not changed from the original one. The results are shown in Table 1. The first column gives the names of the circuits in RevLib [11], except for SteaneEncoding and SteaneErrorDetection. The second and the third columns denote the number of qubits (n), and the gate count (gc) of the circuits, respectively. The following columns show the number of SWAP gates and run-time for the conversion by the naive method and the proposed method.

As can be observed from Table 1, in some cases, a naive method cannot find the best solution. Also, as expected, our method could not deal with a large problem; the quantum circuit, add8_173, in Table 1 could not be converted to an LNN circuit by the proposed method because of the memory explosion. Let (the number of qubits-1) be M, and the depth of the breadth first search to find the best solution be d. Then, the space complexity of the proposed method is obviously $O(M^d)$. Therefore, when the depth of the breadth first search to find the best solution increases, its space complexity increases exponentially. By considering this and the experimental results, we can observe that our method may be able to find the best solution when we need to insert SWAP gates up to around 35 or so. For this reason, if the converted LNN circuit need many SWAP gates, it is not practical to use our proposed method; we may need a heuristic search method.

For the quantum circuits, 3_17_15, decode24, fredkin_5 in Table 1, the numbers of SWAP gates of the naive method and the proposed method are the same. The reason can be seen in their gate dependence graphs. For example, see the gate dependence graph

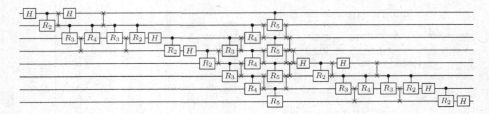

Fig. 16. The LNN AQFT circuit by the method by Saeedi et al. [10]

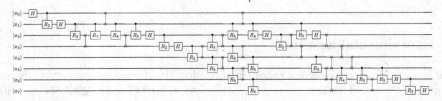

Fig. 17. The LNN AQFT circuit by the proposed method

for *fredkin_5* in Fig. 15, it is observed that we can only change the order of B and C, and/or F and G. Thus, there is no much difference between the naive method and the proposed method.

To show the above (3), we compared the results of converting the AQFT circuit with the state-of-the-art existing method by Saeedi et al. [10]. As described in Sec. 1, the original LNN circuit for AQFT [5] has been improved by the method [9], and then by Saeedi et al. [10]. Fig. 16 shows the LNN circuit for AQFT by Saeedi et al. [10] which has been considered to be the best. Fig 17 shows an LNN circuit for AQFT by our proposed method. As can be seen, the gate order is a bit changed, and the SWAP gates are reduced; The numbers of SWAP gates used are 20 in the method by Saeedi et al. and 18 in our proposed method, respectively.

5   Conclusions

In this paper, we have proposed how to convert a non-LNN quantum circuit into an LNN circuit with the smallest number of SWAP gates by considering the gate order. When the number of SWAP gates is small, the proposed method is able to find the optimum conversion easily with considering the gate order. The experiments show that our method can reduce the number of SWAP gates by two compared to the LNN AQFT circuit converted by the method by Saeedi et al. .

However, if the number of SWAP gates is large, the space complexity increases exponentially. Thus, to convert a large quantum circuit to an LNN circuit in reasonable time, we first need to divide the circuit into small partial circuits, and then apply the proposed method to each partial circuit one by one. Another way to convert a large non-LNN circuit is a heuristic conversion method; it would be an interesting to develop a heuristic.

Because our problem formulation can be seen as a search problem on a graph, we may be able to utilize an idea of the existing traversal algorithms for our purpose.

Acknowledgement. This research was partially supported by Kayamori Foundation of Informational Science Advancement.

References

1. Nielsen, M.A., Chuang, I.L.: Quantum Computation and Quantum Information. Cambridge University Press (2000)
2. Shor, P.W.: Polynomial-time algorithms for prime factorization and discrete logarithms on a quantum computer. SIAM J. Comput. 26, 1484–1509 (1997)
3. Ross, M., Oskin, M.: Quantum computing. Commun. ACM 51(7), 12–13 (2008)
4. Fowler, A.G., Devitt, S.J., Hollenberg, L.C.: Implementation of shor's algorithm on a linear nearest neighbour qubit array. Quantum Information and Computation 4(4), 4:237–4:251 (2004)
5. Takahashi, Y., Kunihiro, N., Ohta, K.: The quantum fourier transform on a linear nearest neighbor architecture. Quantum Information and Computation 7(4), 383–391 (2007)
6. Kutin, S.A.: Shor's algorithm on a nearest-neighbor machine. Technical report, Asian Conference on Quantum Information Science (2007)
7. Choi, B.S., Meter, R.V.: Effects of interaction distance on quantum addition circuits. ArXiv e-prints (September 2008)
8. Fowler, A.G., Hill, C.D., Hollenberg, L.C.L.: Quantum-error correction on linear-nearest-neighbor qubit arrays. Phys. Rev. A 69(4), 042314 (2004)
9. Hirata, Y., Nakanishi, M., Yamashita, S., Nakashima, Y.: An efficient coversion o quantum circuits to a linear nearest neighbor architecture. Qnantum Information and Computation 11(1), 142–166 (2011)
10. Saeedi, M., Wille, R., Drechsler, R.: Synthesis of quantum circuits for linear nearest neighbor architectures. Quantum Information Processing, 1–23 (2010), 10.1007/s11128-010-0201-2
11. Wille, R., Große, D., Teuber, L., Dueck, G.W., Drechsler, R.: RevLib: An online resource for reversible functions and reversible circuits. In: International Symposium on Multiple Valued Logic, pp. 220–225 (May 2008)

Towards the Limits of Cascaded Reversible (Quantum-Inspired) Circuits

Stéphane Burignat[1], Mariusz Olczak[1], Michał Klimczak[1], and Alexis De Vos[1,2]

[1] Universiteit Gent, Vakgroep Elektronica en Informatiesystemen,
Sint Pietersnieuwstraat 41, 9000 Gent, Belgium
research@burignat.eu
[2] Imec v.z.w.,
Kapeldreef 75, 3001 Leuven, Belgium
alex@elis.ugent.be

Abstract. Several prototypes and proofs of concept of reversible (quantum-inspired) digital circuits have been successfully realized these last years, proving that *digital reversible dual-line pass-transistor technology* may be used for reversible linear computations. In order for this new technology to be used in commercial applications, several questions have to be answerd first. In particular, the number of gates possibly cascaded, the maximum reachable frequency, the maximum acceptable delays and amplitude drops are the key issues discussed in this paper.

1   Introduction

Because conventional restoring computing is based on logically-irreversible elementary operations that lead to information destruction and increase of entropy [1,2], reversible logic has been developed. Different synthesis approaches for reversible computation have been developed [3,4,5]. Hardware applying *reversible adiabatic dual-line pass-transistor CMOS* circuits have been proved to be energetically economic, allowing to divide by about a factor twenty, the energy consumption of a given linear function [6]. In other words, 95 % of the energy input during computation, is recovered during the uncomputation.

This is made possible, for the biases are only used for substrate and wells polarization. The necessary energy used for computation is only supplied by the input signals. Moreover, the complementary signals ensure that all the signals can be reused in next computation steps, keeping the energy from gate to gate instead of throwing away a large part of the stored energy, as it is the case in conventional restoring electronics.

The latter circuits being directly connected to biases, they have access to a large reservoir of energy, such that, at each clock cycle, fast switches can occur, boosted by the important quantity of charges injected into the gates. In reversible circuits, things are different as the goal is to have smooth enough transitions for the charges to be reinjected in the circuit, such that the computations are thermodynamically-reversible [1,7].

A. De Vos and R. Wille (Eds.): RC 2011, LNCS 7165, pp. 102–111, 2012.
© Springer-Verlag Berlin Heidelberg 2012

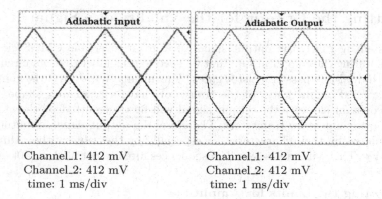

Channel_1: 412 mV	Channel_1: 412 mV
Channel_2: 412 mV	Channel_2: 412 mV
time: 1 ms/div	time: 1 ms/div

Fig. 1. Experimental measurements of one dual input and one dual output of the Cuccaro adder in reverse calculation (subtraction)

Dual-line adiabatic triangular pulses have already been successfully used in full-adders [8] and in a 4-bits Cuccaro adder [9,10] composed of gates proposed by [11] and [12]. To have optimal switching, a specific adiabatic pulse shape is mandatory to accurately perform calculations in an adiabatic dynamics [10]. These pulses may either be triangles as illustated in Fig.1, trapezes or sinus.

In this work, only triangular and sinus pulses are used in order to evaluate the performance limits of reversible circuits, but some other signals using smooth enough transitions may be used for applications. As for example, the trapezoidal-shape signal holding the extreme values of a triangular pulse for a short time, has been used in one application aiming at interfacing a 4-bits reversible Cuccaro adder with a Xilinx FPGA [13]. Another interesting shape would be to use sinus for transitions instead of linear slopes. Of course, to generate such pulse would be a little bit more complicated but may allow to push away the limits obtained in this paper as later discussed.

Sinusoidal waveforms have been proposed for the clocking signals in energy-recovering logic [14,15,16,17]. In the present paper, we discuss reversible circuits which have no clocking. The sinusoidal pulses used here, are digital input signals instead.

In the first part, we will discuss the validity of the used signals, according to their amplitude and relative delays. In the second part, the limit number of gates possibly cascaded will be evaluated, both when triangular adiabatic or sinus adiabatic pulses are used.

We stress that both, the numerical simulation and the experimental measurements concern standard CMOS circuits, i.e. circuits in a technology developed for standard restoring logic. This technology is not optimized for pass-transistor logic, let alone for reversible logic. As an example, large values of threshold voltages (V_T) are beneficial for restoring logic, but cause problems in reversible computing: a large V_T reduces the pulse widths of signals and as a consequence, reduces the window of allowed delays for output signals.

2 Setting the Criteria for the Validity of a Signal

As stressed by Fig.1, the output signal of a given reversible CMOS circuit is modified during the computation. First we need to remember that our circuits are built with dual-line pass-transistor gates. This means that even if the command signals applied on the gates of the transistors have a triangular shape – thus having constant slopes – the output signal will be transmitted by the channels of these complementary transistors. Therefore, the output signal amplitude will be modulated by their characteristics, especially by the value of their threshold voltage V_T. This will have several consequences already detailed in [10].

2.1 Setting the Limits for Amplitudes

For our present study, let's remark that the output signal is narrowed, as long as the command pulse remains lower than the threshold voltage V_T of the transistors. The signal will then become significant, only at the moment the command signal is larger than V_T, which unfortunately is about 0.3 V. Then, a sharp transition occurs, until the output voltage catches up with the input voltage, reduced by a small voltage drop in the channel impedances of the transmission gates. The command potential for which the output signal is restored is about $V_{c_0} = 420$ mV, both for the transmission gates and for the Cuccaro adder [10].

As both, the command and the signal to be transmitted are, in the reversible circuit, coming from the inputs, they should both have about the same initial amplitude, even if this is not mandatory. In order the circuit to be able to perform correct calculations, all the signals in the circuit should have an amplitude at least superior to the minimum defined voltage output $V_{c_0} = 420$ mV.

If we consider that some parasitic signals may be superimposed, we should fix an even larger minimum voltage limit, for the signals to be acceptable for applications. We will therefore arbitrarily fix this limit to $V_{o_{min}} = 0.5$ V, which allows parasitic signals as large as 80 mV. Let us notice that these values are set up when a mean value of 0 V is used, and when positive voltages stand for a logic "1" and negative voltages for a logic "0". Otherwise, these values will define the gap to the mean value.

2.2 Setting the Limits for Delays

In a reversible circuit, if the number of transmission gates passed by a signal is different from the number for another signal, at the end of the computation, some delay may appear between the two pulses, possibly introducing calculation errors [10]. This problem is related to the so-called glitches in conventional electronics. Moreover, high frequencies will also add extra delays making the situation worse.

Exerimentally, the Cuccaro adder is empacked in a dual-in-line package which is simply placed on a bread-board with unshielded wires used for connecting the inputs. Such a set-up is of course far from optimal to perform frequency measurements as a lot of external parasitic capacitances are added to the circuit itself. Nevertheless, frequencies as high as a few megahertz can still be reached.

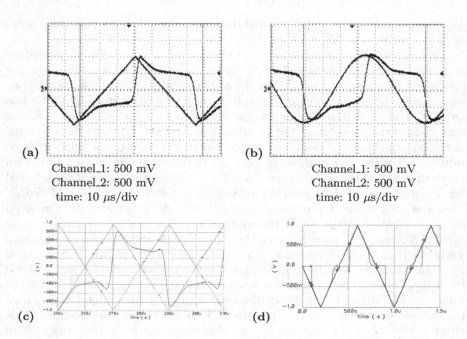

(a) Channel_1: 500 mV
Channel_2: 500 mV
time: 10 μs/div

(b) Channel_1: 500 mV
Channel_2: 500 mV
time: 10 μs/div

Fig. 2. (a) Experimental impact of the measurement probe on the computed output signal when an adiabatic triangular pulse is used, and (b) when an adiabatic sinusoidal pulse is applied, both at a frequency of 14 kHz. (c) Similar impact of the probe on the computed output signal obtained by simulation of a higher frequency of 50 kHz and (d) simulated output without probe at a frequency of 5 MHz; the signal is, in this latter case, still well defined.

The upper experimental limit for frequency, which can be reached on our set-up while still having *usable* signals, is about 14 kHz, as seen in Fig.2a when an adiabatic triangular pulse is used and Fig.2b using a sinusoidal one. In a simulation, similar results are obtained only if a virtual probe is placed at output Fig.2c; otherwise, results are similar to those of Fig.1. This difference is explained by the introduction, at the measured output, of an extra capacitance of 32 pF caused by the probe.

In Fig.2d, simulating 5 MHz adiabatic signals without the presence of such capacitance, the output signal is still triangular adiabatic, as expected. The impact of the increased frequency can be seen in the delay added to the beginning time of the transition slope, when the pass-transistor gate starts to conduct the output signal. The sharply raising slope is delayed, narrowing the output pulse at its raising side.

Therefore, we can start answering the question of validity of a signal. As we can see in these latter cases, the computation can still be done without error if the levels are large enough to be detected without any confusion and if at each gate, between the command signal and the transmitted signal, a maximum delay of 25 % is respected [10].

If the capacitance placed in series at the output is large, this will introduce important extra capacitance effects as in Fig.2a and b. This would also be the case if several gates are cascaded or if one circuit is cascaded with another one presenting a large input capacitance. But, would these output signals be bad anyway? This capacitance maintains the output voltage above 500 mV for more than 25 % of the period time, but less than half a period. In effect, the new value of the output signal will force the output either to switch to the opposite logic value – as it is the case in these figures –, or to the same value with a transition in the direction of the mean value – to follow the adiabatic-shape of the injected input signals, even if the corresponding voltage is not always reached. Moreover, even if at each single step of the computation the delay between the command signal of a gate and the signal transmitted by this same gate remains shorter than 25 %, the total delay between the input signals and the output signals of a whole circuit – such as the Cuccaro adder – may be substantially larger than 25 %. In this latter case, the output signals would remain still valid and usable if the delays between them are small enough such that a reading time of the output values may be defined. This is possible only if this maximum delay between all the outputs is smaller than the time the first output signal is well defined. This latter criterion for large circuits, is somewhat more restrictive than the 25 % of the period previously proposed for simple gates and small circuits.

2.3   Criteria for the Validity of a Signal

As a conclusion, to be valid, the signal should have the following characteristics:

1. each signal should have a minimum amplitude of 500 mV,
2. at each gate, the delay between the command pulse and the transmitted one should be inferior to the time the command signal is well-defined and in all cases inferior to 25 % of the period,
3. the maximum delay between all the outputs of a full circuit should be smaller than the time the first computed output signal, is well defined.

3   The Limit Number of Cascaded Gates

The criteria for good signal defined, we now have the tools to evaluate the effective numbers of possible cascaded gates. We already experimentally evaluated that it should be possible to cascade more than 20 Cuccaro adders at a low frequency of 120 Hz, while a probe is connected to the output [10].

In this section, we will present simulation results performed on a simple chain of cascaded gates, both pass-transistor gates and controlled-NOT gates and using triangular adiabatic pulses. The number of cascaded gates used, ranges from 1 up to 80. The frequency range, lays between 1 MHz and 10 MHz. At each output, an *"ideal"* probe will be considered, formed by a 1 MΩ resistor placed in parallel with a 1 aF capacitor, which is close to an integrated open wire and that present a cutoff frequency of 1 THz. Simulations are performed using the Cadence™ Spectre© electrical simulator. The models of the transistors come from the 350 nm technology standard library from ON Semiconductor, already successfully used for simulating our Cuccaro adder [10].

Controlled-NOT (CNOT) gates are composed of four transmission gates (TG) [8]. Each input signal to be transmitted, *"sees"* two transmission gates in parallel: one is transmitting the signal and the other one is stopping it, acting as an open circuit. Each command signal will then *"see"*, twice as much transistor gates in the case of CNOT gates than for TG. In other words, at first order, twice as many capacitances are to be taken into account for CNOT gates. In reality, the situation is even more complex, as all the equivalent resistors and capacitances present in the models of the complementary transistors should be taken into account.

Also, some differences are found depending on the polarity of the signals to be considered. In effect, the transmission gates are built using two complementary transistors. Each one of them is transmitting the signal which has the opposite value than the signal applied on its transistor gate. As for example, the n-type transistor, which is active when a *positive* signal is applied on its gate, cannot conduct a signal of same polarity. Otherwise, the transistor will switch to a non-active position, as all its contacts are at the same potential. The same is found for the p-type transistor when *negative* signals are involved. Therefore, the n-type transistor will transmit only negative signals whereas the p-type transistor will pass only positive signals[1].

As the two complementary transistors do not have the same sizes, in order to compensate the difference between the mobility of the carriers involved, the p-type transistor is at least three times wider than the n-type transistor. Therefore, larger capacitances are introduced by the p-type transistor. Hence, if we can consider the transconductance g_{DS} of the two types of transistor as equivalent, it is definitely not the case for the different capacitance values that are then larger for the p-type transistors.

We then, can expect some differences between the results obtained with cascaded transmission-gates compared to CNOT gates; as the total capacitance seen by a signal is different in each case.

Simulations of Fig.3, present the variations of the delays between the command pulse and the transmited signal, and the voltage drop of output signals, as a function of the number of cascaded gates and of the frequency. The number **N** of cascaded gates used for simulations are [1, 2, 3, 4, 8, 16, 20, 24, 28, 32, 40], whereas the used frequencies **f** are [1, 2, 3.3, 5, 10] MHz.

Fig.3a is presenting the simulated variation of the delays obtained between the transmitted signals and the command pulse, as a function of the number of cascaded gates. As expected, we found a smaller delay for TG compared to CNOT gates. The latter are close to be the double of the delays obtained for TG.

---

[1] *Positive* and *negative* signals are to be considered relatively to the mean value of the adiabatic signal. In this discussion, the mean value V_{mean} is supposed to be 0 V.

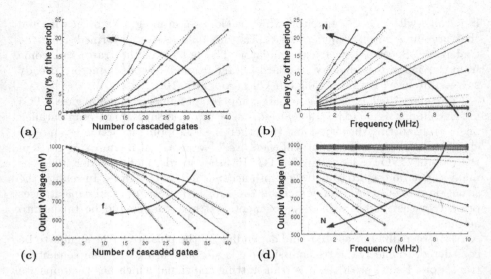

Fig. 3. Simulations of cascaded gates:
(- -) controlled-NOT gates.
The used number **N** of cascaded gates are [1, 2, 3, 4, 8, 16, 20, 24, 28, 32, 40].
The used frequencies **f** are [1, 2, 3.3, 5, 10] MHz.
  (a) – Evolution of the delays between outputs, as a function of **N**, for different **f**,
  (b) – Evolution of the delays between outputs, as a function of **f**, for different **N**,
  (c) – Evolution of the output voltage as a function of **N**, for different **f**,
  (d) – Evolution of the output voltage as a function of **f**, for different **N**.

As the cascaded gates may be, at first order, modelized by cascaded first-order low-pass filters – yet dominated by resistive-capacitive effects – this factor 2 may be related to the digital propagation delay $\tau = (R.C)/2$ of the filters; R is the equivalent resistor of the gates (filters) and C their equivalent capacitance. The equivalent capacitance "seen" by the signals passing the CNOT gates being close to the double of the TG's ones, the characteristic time τ is then logically found to be of same proportion.

Also, some differences are found between TG and CNOT, for the variation of amplitude drop as a function of the number of cascaded gates, as presented in Fig.3c. Once again, the voltage drop is smaller for TG than for CNOTs.

The delays appear to be function of N^{α}, with $\alpha = 2$, as attested by the linearity of the curves while using log-log scales.

Both the delay and the voltage drop variations, appear to be "quasi"-linear on a large range of frequencies, as shown respectively in Fig.3b and 3d. This is true, both for the transmission gates and for the controlled-NOTs.

This is coherent with the model for delays proposed by [18] for RC ladder circuits. If we consider all the cascade gates as identical, according to [18], we obtain a time constant $\tau = R.C.\left((N+1)(2N+1)\right)/6$, which is a quadratic function of N, and a total delay proportional to the frequency $\Delta = \Delta_0.f.\tau$, where Δ_0 is a constant.

From the physics, another estimation may be done. If we consider the size of the n-type transistors to be approximately $S \simeq 350 \times 500$ nm^2 with an oxide thickness of about $t_{ox} \simeq 10$ nm, then, the estimated capacitance for each transistor would be about $C = (\epsilon_0.\epsilon_{ox}.S)/t_{ox} \simeq 6.10^{-16}$ F, where $\epsilon_0 \simeq 8.85.10^{-12}$ F/m is the vaccum permittivity, $\epsilon_{ox} = 3.9$ is the dielectric constant of the SiO$_2$, $t_{ox} \simeq 10$ nm is the oxide thickness. P-type transistor capacitance would be about three times bigger. Moreover, as each transmission gate has an equivalent resistor of about $R = 8$ kΩ [10], the cutoff frequency may be evaluated according to physical basis to about 129 MHz for 16 cascaded transmission gates, if only n-type transistors are involved. On this basis, we can evaluate the theoretical cutoff frequency for 16 cascaded CNOT gates around 64 MHz for the 350 nm CMOS technology and divide those two values by a factor 3 to take into account the limitation brought by the p-type transistor, that has a three times wider channel – and by the way, a three times larger capacitance. Therefore, a cutoff frequency of 10 MHz would limitate the number of CNOT gates to about 57 if only n-type transistors are involved, or 33 if using only p-type transistors. Actually, 40 is the maximum number of CNOT gates, according to simulations.

4   Discussion on the Positive Impact of a Lower V_T

Non-standard CMOS processes, e.g. the SOI (Silicon On Insulator) technology, make low-V_T circuits possible. Such reduced V_T would allow lowering the minimal necessary voltage for the signals to be well defined. In other words, the amplitude of a signal needed to be representative of the desired logical data would be smaller.

Of course, it is possible, even in the context of this study, to allow a signal to be smaller in amplitude, than the threshold voltage. But this would also increase the risk of having unwanted pulses when some oscillations appear at the moment the charges are transferred from one transistor to another or from one gate to another. These oscillations may be of the two polarities, yet introducing wrong informations. The moment these oscillations appear is, of course, correlated with the moment one transistor starts to conduct, i.e. when the command voltage on the transistor gate reaches the V_T[2]. Therefore, if very small V_T are used, some extra criteria should be added, in particular for higher frequencies where the oscillations are getting bigger.

A lower V_T would also allow to enlarge the signal pulses, bringing wider windows for synchronizing the signals. The number of possible cascaded gates would then be augmented both because the minimal amplitude would be reduced and because the allowed delay would be increased.

---

[2] This phenomenon has not been discussed here, as it is related to the ability of a circuit to recover, during the uncomputation step, a large part of the energy used during computation.

5   Conclusion

In this work, we first discuss in details, the "criteria for good signal" in reversible computation, in particular, the criteria for allowed delays and amplitudes. We also pointed out, the fact that the use of threshold voltages smaller than the one used in conventional restoring technology, would increase the possible number of cascaded gates, giving the possibility to design even larger reversible circuits. In the second part, we presented a detailed study on the simulated evolution of output delays and pulse amplitudes, both as a function of the number of cascaded gates and of the frequency. This study shows that it is possible to cascade a lot of reversible gates, but also, that the size of the final circuit will strongly depend on the frequency at which the computation should be done.

Acknowledgement. The authors thank the Danish Council for Strategic Research for support of this work in the framework of the MICROPOWER research project and the TECHNICAL UNIVERSITY OF ŁÓDŹ for collaboration through *Erasmus Exchanges*.

References

1. Landauer, R.: Irreversibility and heat generation in the computing process. IBM Journal of Research and Development 5(3), 183–191 (1961)
2. Von Neumann, J.: Theory of self-reproducing automata, p. 66ss. University of Illinois Press, Urbana (1966)
3. Markov, I.: An introduction to reversible circuits. In: Proceedings of the 12th International Workshop on Logic and Synthesis, Laguna Beach, pp. 318–319 (May 2003)
4. Wille, R., Drechsler, R.: BDD-based synthesis of reversible logic for large functions. In: Proceedings of the 46th Design Automation Conference, San Francisco, pp. 270–275 (July 2009)
5. Wille, R., Drechsler, R.: Towards a design flow for reversible logic, 184 pages. Springer, Heidelberg (2010) ISBN:978-90-481-9578-7
6. Van Rentergem, Y., De Vos, A.: Reversible full adders applying Fredkin gates. In: Proceedings of the 12th International Conference on MIXed DESign of Integrated Circuits and Systems (MIXDES), Kraków, pp. 179–184 (June 2005)
7. Bennett, C.H.: Logical reversibility of computation. IBM Journal of Research and Development 17(6), 525–532 (1973)
8. De Vos, A.: Reversible computing, 249 pages. Wiley-VCH (2010) ISBN:978-3-527-40992-1
9. Cuccaro, S., Draper, T., Moulton, D., Kutin, S.: A new quantum ripple-carry addition circuit. In: Proceedings of the 8th Workshop on Quantum Information Processing, Cambridge (June 2005); arXiv:quant-ph/0410184v1, 9 pages (2004)
10. Burignat, S., De Vos A.: Test of a majority-based reversible (quantum) 4 bits ripple-carry adder in adiabatic calculation. In: Proceedings of the 18th International Conference on MIXed DESign of Integrated Circuits and Systems (MIXDES), Gliwice, Poland, pp. 368–373 (2011)
11. Feynman, R.P.: Quantum mechanical computer. Optics News 11, 11–20 (1985)

12. Fredkin, E., Toffoli, T.: Conservative logic. International Journal of Theoretical Physics 21, 219–253 (2004)
13. Burignat, S., Thomsen, M.K., Klimczak, M., Olczak, M., De Vos, A.: Interfacing Reversible Pass-Transistor CMOS Chips with Conventional Restoring CMOS Circuits. In: De Vos, A., Wille, R. (eds.) RC 2011. LNCS, vol. 7165, pp. 113–123. Springer, Heidelberg (2012)
14. Oklobdžija, V.G., Maksimović, D., Lin, F.: Pass-transistor adiabatic logic using single power-clock supply. IEEE Transactions on Circuits and Systems II: Analog and Digital Signal Processing 44(10), 842–846 (1997)
15. Lim, J., Kim, D.-G., Chae, S.-I.: A 16-bit carry-lookahead adder using reversible energy recovery logic for ultra-low-energy systems. IEEE Journal of Solid-State Circuits 34(6), 898–903 (1999)
16. Hang, G., Wu, X.: Improved structure for adiabatic CMOS circuits design. Microelectronics Journal 33, 403–407 (2002)
17. Ziesler, C.H., Kim, J., Papaefthymiou, M.C.: Energy recovering ASIC design. In: Proceedings of the IEEE Computer Society Annual Symposium on VLSI, Tampa, pp. 133–138 (2003)
18. Alioto, M., Palumbo, G., Poli, M.: Evaluation of energy consumption in RC ladder circuits driven by a ramp input. IEEE Transactions on Very Large Scale Integration (VLSI) Systems 12(10), 1094–1107 (2004)

Interfacing Reversible Pass-Transistor CMOS Chips with Conventional Restoring CMOS Circuits

Stéphane Burignat[1], Michael Kirkedal Thomsen[2],
Michał Klimczak[1], Mariusz Olczak[1], and Alexis De Vos[1,3]

[1] Universiteit Gent, Vakgroep Elektronica en Informatiesystemen,
Sint Pietersnieuwstraat 41, 9000 Gent, Belgium
[2] University of Copenhagen, Department of Computer Science, DIKU,
Universitetsparken 1, 2100 Copenhagen, Denmark
[3] Imec v.z.w.,
Kapeldreef 75, 3001 Leuven, Belgium
research@burignat.eu, shapper@diku.dk, alex@elis.ugent.be

Abstract. Recent progress on the prototyping of reversible digital circuits, have shown that *adiabatic reversible dual-line pass-transistor logic* can be used for special purpose applications in reversible computation. This, however, raises new issues regarding the compatibility between this adiabatic logic implementation and conventional CMOS logic. The greatest difficulty is brought by the difference in signal shape used by these two logic families. Whereas standard switching CMOS circuits are operated by rectangular pulses, dual-line pass-transistor reversible circuits are controlled by triangular or trapezoidal signals to ensure adiabatic switching of the transistors. This work proposes a simple technical solution that allows interfacing reversible pass-transistor logic with conventional CMOS logic, represented here by an FPGA embedded in a commercial Xilinx Spartan-3E board. All proposed solutions have successfully been tested, which enables the FPGA to perform calculations directly on a reversible chip.

1 Introduction

Conventional computing is based on logically irreversible elementary operations, which leads to information destruction and an increase in entropy [1,2]. Eliminating the irreversibility of computations *is* possible. It was first shown by Bennett [3], whome theoretically enabled calculation processes with zero energy dissipation at finite speed. At the circuit level, this is only possible using reversible logical "machines" that perform thermodynamically reversible computations. Such "machines" have been conceptually proposed by Fredkin and Toffoli [4] and later extended for a quantum mechanics based computational model by *eg.* Feynman [5]. CMOS implementations of these logic operators were proposed by De Vos *et al.* [6] using dual-line pass-transistor (DLPT) circuits.

A. De Vos and R. Wille (Eds.): RC 2011, LNCS 7165, pp. 112–122, 2012.
© Springer-Verlag Berlin Heidelberg 2012

This CMOS dual-line pass-transistor technology is demonstrated to be energetically efficient; results of simulations show energy consumption down to only 5 % of conventional CMOS [7]. In effect, biases are only used for substrate and wells polarization, while the necessary energy used for computation is brought only by the input signals. Moreover, the complementary signals ensure that the charge flowing in the circuits can be reused at next step of the computation, instead of being thrown away as in conventional restoring electronics. By opposition, restoring electronics makes use of biases to perform the computation and restore the signal at the same time, throwing away a large amount of energy at each clock cycle.

Whereas the classical digital CMOS switching technology uses square-wave waveforms to define logic "0" and logic "1", DLPT with adiabatic switching necessitates two complementary signals. Furthermore, it is mandatory that the two signals change gradually to ensure accurate adiabatic switching of the circuits [8] (see Fig. 1(a)). These signals are often triangular or trapezoidal waveforms. We refer to these signals by the name *adiabatic signals*.

Another advantage of adiabatic signals, is that these also avoid calculation errors, possibly caused by delays appearing between signals when classical rectangular shape signals involve steep transition slopes. The undesired pulses are then filtered when the smooth triangular slope amplitude is lower than the threshold voltage of the pass-transistor gates, thereby lowering the undesired artifacts [8] (output pulse shown in Fig. 1(b)).

We expect that, in its first "commercial" applications, reversible electronics will appear in ASICs and will be embedded in an environment of conventional CMOS circuits. Interfacing irreversible restoring logic and adiabatic logic has been proposed by Amirante *et al.* [9]. But their implementation is based on a different adiabatic logic family, by which their results can not be transfered directly to the reversible DLPT logic we are using. In this work, we propose a solution for interfacing a commercial FPGA, first with a reversible CMOS reversible binary adder [8,10,11] and then later with a reversible ALU [12]. First, in Sect. 2 we present the possibilities and the limitations caused by the Xilinx Spartan 3E FPGA [13]. Then, in Sect. 3 the proposed technical electronic solutions are detailed. Finally in Sect. 4 we conclude.

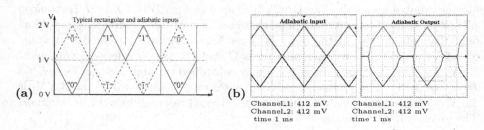

Fig. 1. (a) Typical square-wave and adiabatic dual-line inputs. (b) Experimental measurements of one dual input and one dual output using the a reversible binary adder in reverse calculation.

2   FPGA Capabilities and Limitations

Modern FPGA boards are much more than a simple chip of programmable hardware with a small memory and a parallel port to load the program. Even smaller FPGA starter-boards include a wide range of connector devices, which can be interfaced directly from the FPGA in a more or less simple way.

For the purpose of connecting the reversible chip with a digital circuit, it suffices to use an FPGA with a low number of logic cells. Therefore, the cheap (less than 200 euros) Xilinx Spartan®-3E FPGA Starter Kit Board from Digilent is used for this proof-of-concept. This board has a large number of input and output devices, a good manual, and, as it is a popular starter board, it is easy to find example implementations of device interfaces in both VHDL and Verilog. The on-board devices we are using are

- the clock generator: the standard clock source with a frequency of 50 MHz,
- the DAC: the digital-to-analog convertor, used to generate the adiabatic signals for the reversible chip inputs,
- the FX2 100-pin expansion connector for connecting the digital inputs and outputs to the connector board,
- the LCD display, used to show the results of the calculations, and
- the buttons, switches and the knob for controlling the board while executing.

The detailed use of each device will be described in the following sections.

2.1   Signal Generation

The adiabatic signal is normally generated with an accurate full-wave rectifier connected to a waveform generator [8]. This setup ensures a powerful and precise signal that is necessary for performing accurate measurements, but the setup is too big to be used in computers and especially small devices. This work only focuses on interfacing the reversible chip with classical CMOS circuits. We therefore need to ensure that the functionality of the reversible chip is correct, while the full computing circuit still gains the benefits of the reversible chip and the adiabatic switching. We use the DAC (included on the FPGA board) to generate the adiabatic signals. The DAC (presented in Fig. 2) is a *Lineal Technology LTC2624*. It has four outgoing pins, that can be controlled individually or all at once. By default, two of the outputs (pins A and B) have a reference[1] voltage of 3.3 V, while the two other pins (pins C and D) have a reference voltage of 2.5 V. The DAC output voltage is linearly controlled through a *Serial Peripheral Interface* (SPI). The accessible voltage values range between 0 V and 3.3 V or 2.5 V depending on the chosen pin and a value represented by a 12 bit number. The given voltage accuracy is 5 %.

---

[1] The default reference voltages of the DAC can be changed, but this requires desoldering of two resistors, and direct interfacing of two pins. Therefore, we have chosen to use the default settings.

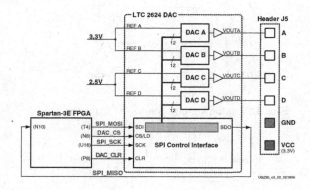

Fig. 2. Schematic of the digital to analog converter. *Figure adapted from [13].*

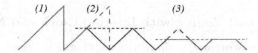

Fig. 3. Generation of the trapezoid signal for adiabatic switching

Often, a triangular waveform is used for adiabatic switching. But, as we will see in Sect. 2.2, it can be beneficial to use a trapezoidal shape instead. The steps to generate both these waveforms are illustrated in Fig. 3. First, we make a saw-tooth by incrementing a value in each clock cycle *(1)*. By doing the incrementing modulo some maximum number[2] we have the sudden value drop that is a characteristic of the saw-tooth waveform. Second step, is to make a triangular waveform and this is done by subtracting the most significant half of the saw-tooth waveform from the least significant half *(2)*. Finally, the trapezoidal waveform is obtained by removing the tops from the triangular waveform *(3)*. This is a simple greater-than check and the upper limit can be used to control the slope of the trapezoid waveform.

The period of the adiabatic signals are, of course, limited by the DAC. For each change of voltage level by the DAC, we need to send a 32-bit value through the SPI. Four FPGA clock cycles are needed in order to send each bit. As about 50 points are necessary to generate a well-defined adiabatic waveform for each of the two DAC outputs, and because the FPGA runs at 50 MHz, then the maximum reachable frequency for the adiabatic signal is about 4 kHz. This is not much, but it is fast enough for this proof-of-concept, which aims to show the possibility to interface the two technologies.

---

[2] The modulo 2^n operation is done automatically when using an *n*-bit adder circuit.

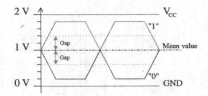

Fig. 4. Analog signals generated from the DAC

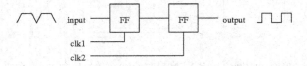

Fig. 5. Two-level memory interfacing the adiabatic input and the digital output signals

2.2   Interfacing and Timing with Internal Clock and Memory

The adiabatic waveforms are periodical and, therefore, have a build-in clock period. Moreover, both the digital circuits and the reversible chip must communicate at the same frequency[3]. Setting the phases between the signals from the FPGA and the adiabatic signal is not obvious when we want the circuits to run in a correct adiabatic way. We need to pay particular attention to the interfacing between the adiabatic signal and the conventional memory.

For the adiabatic signal a logic value is well-defined, either if its amplitude voltage exceeds the mean value by a quarter of the total signal range, or if it reduces by the same voltage gap (illustrated in Fig. 4). If trapezoidal waveforms are used then the signals are best defined during the constant plateau situated between the raising and falling transitions. If triangular waveforms are used, then the signal is best defined during a shorter time ranging from half the raising time to half the falling time of the triangular waveforms.

This is in contrast to digital circuits, where the well-defined logic values are situated just before the clock ticks and the logic value is changed. It is therefore not possible to make an interface with a single memory element and an approach using a two-level memory as in Fig. 5 must be applied.

The idea is that the first flip-flop reads the adiabatic signal at the clearest logic value, while the second flip-flop is updated at the change of the adiabatic signal. This interfacing works best if we are using a trapezoidal waveform, as these can be interpreted at their constant plateau as either digital logic "1" or a digital logic "0".

To have an optimal timing between the two flip-flops, we must therefore have two separate internal clock signals. Using more clock signals to control energy-efficient circuits with adiabatic switching, is not a new idea. The *split-level charge*

---

[3] Other parts of the FPGA, such as the generation of the adiabatic signal and control of devices, will run with the standard 50 MHz clock.

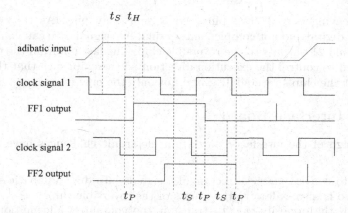

Fig. 6. Detailed timing of the interface between adiabatic signal and memory. t_S is the setup time, t_H the hold time, and t_P the propagation time of the memory.

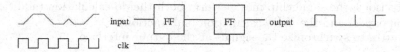

Fig. 7. Simplified interfacing with a single clock signal that is in-phase with the period of the adiabatic signal. The first flip-flop is updated at rising clock-edge whereas the second one at falling clock-edge.

recovery logic (SCRL) [14], which was used to implement the Pendulum processor [15], is controlled with up to 7 different clock signals. Both in SCRL and in our approach timing of the clock signals are essential. Therefore, we must consider the setup time, hold time, and propagation delay of the memory.

Fig. 6 illustrates a detailed timing diagram. This diagram does not consider signal propagation in the combinatorial circuits that has to be added to the minimum clock period. The figure is only intended to show that the trapezoidal adiabatic signal can uphold the timing constraint of the digital memory, while still ensuring adiabatic switching.

In the current setup, the maximum frequency of the adiabatic waveform is many times larger than the time constraints of the FPGA memory and the detailed timing is, therefore, not necessary. It is acceptable to make a simplified implementation with a single clock signal that is in-phase with the period of the adiabatic signal (shown in Fig. 7). The first flip-flop is updated at the rising clock-edge, where there is a clear adiabatic signal while the second flip-flop is updated at the falling clock-edge, where the adiabatic signal is switching.

2.3   I/O Programming

To transfer the input and output values for reversible circuits from/to the FPGA, a 100-pin Hirose FX2 connector is used. Most of these 100 pins have a special purpose, leaving only 38 I/O pins and 5 input-only pins. As the connecting signals are digital and not complementary dual-line signals, we can control up to 21 inputs and 21 outputs to the reversible chip. The last pin from the connector will be used to control the execution direction on the chip, such that the FPGA can exploit the chip's reversibility, and not only the energy savings.

3   The Interface Board

In the design of the interface board, four electronic challenges have to be addressed.

- First, to convert classical rectangular signals into dual adiabatic signals, in order to transmit data to the inputs of the reversible chip.
- Second, the opposite, *i.e.* to transmit the computed information back to the FPGA in the form of a classical rectangular signal, starting from the dual-line adiabatic outputs of the chip.
- Third, to exploit the reversibility of the chip by making computation in both directions; the same chip may perform both the do-calculation (addition in this paper) and the undo-calculation (subtraction).
- Fourth, to synchronize the signals at the output interface.

3.1   Bringing the FPGA Commands to the Reversible Inputs

The conversion from classical square-wave signals to dual-line adiabatic signals (shown in Fig. 8a) can be done using a double $1 \rightarrow 2$ pass-transistor multiplexer: *e.g.* the commercial MUX SN74CBTLV3257. As the multiplexer is made of pass-transistor gates, it can be used in both directions.

The command inputs to the multiplexer are the enable $\overline{oe}$ input and the selection bit **s**. When $\overline{oe}$ is "1", the circuit is placed in high-impedance such that no input signal can be transmitted to output. When $\overline{oe}$ is "0", the selection bit s will act as the control to a switch and redirect the input signal to one of the two outputs. By applying the logical signal coming from the FPGA as the selection bit s, it is possible to connect the input to either output A if $s =$ "0" or else output B if $s =$ "1". Then, by adequately connecting the four outputs to the adiabatic logic "1" and logic "0" for the two first outputs and then logic "0" and logic "1" for the two next, we can obtain the mandatory dual-line adiabatic signals: logic "0" if $s = 0$ and logic "1" if $s = 1$.

The advantage of this solution is that it is already implemented with pass-transistor gates (Fig. 8b). In total, three pass-transistor gates are needed for each data signal coming from the FPGA. Therefore, if one wants to use a reversible circuit as an integrated part of an irreversible restoring logic circuit, this solution can easily be implemented. It will also reduce the number of contacts in the packaging. Even the classical enable $\overline{oe}$ and selection inputs s may be directly used. One only needs to provide the reversible chip with dual signals built at the conventional circuit side using, for example, two inverters to obtain the complementary signal. The two signals s and $\overline{oe}$ can be either constant values or adiabatic signals.

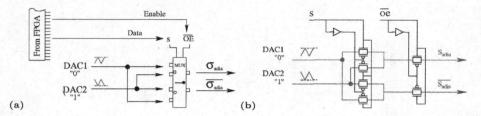

Fig. 8. (**a**) Demultiplexer used as signal converter. The adiabatic signals corresponding to the desired logic value defined by s, are routed from the DACs to the output, by the multiplexer. (**b**) Corresponding schematic using pass-transistor gates.

3.2   Bringing the Results of the Calculation to the FPGA

Remodeling the result represented by the adiabatic signal to a digital square-wave signal for the FPGA is less trivial. It corresponds to implement a threshold detector, which can be done using an operational amplifier. This solution is expensive, both in terms of energy consumption and surface area. In effect, if one of the dual-signal can easily be thrown away or the energy reused by implementing energy-recovering circuits, it will necessitate a buffer for impedance adaption cascaded to an operational amplifier for each signal to be send to the FPGA. This may reduce the interest for implementing reversible circuits, as the surface area or the consumption of this interface becomes bigger than the reversible circuit itself.

Instead, we can interface the adiabatic signal directly with the FPGA, as described in Sect. 2.2. This, of course, raises the question of what to do with the negated value of the dual-line adiabatic signal. To throw it away, as done in the current implementation, would dissipate energy – so perhaps this energy could be harvested with energy-recovering circuits.

3.3   The Problem of Reversibility

Controlling execution direction of the computation is essential in order to exploit the reversibility of the reversible chip, and by this way, choose the function to be performed; in this case an addition or a subtraction. A technical solution for controlling execution direction is again to use $1 \rightarrow 2$ multiplexers to route each line of the adiabatic signals to either an input or an output of the reversible chip.

The schematic in Fig. 9 presents this solution. As previously, the input *enable* allows to isolate the outputs from the inputs of the multiplexer. The *selection* input s is used as a selection bit for the execution direction. This control comes directly from the FPGA, as it is a digital signal.

Each dual-line wire of the input information is routed either to an input or to an output of the reversible chip, depending on the value of s. Our solution is simply to connect the multiplexer's first output to the reversible chip's inputs and the multiplexer's second output to the reversible chip's outputs. The inverse is done to read the computed information: the multiplexer's second output is

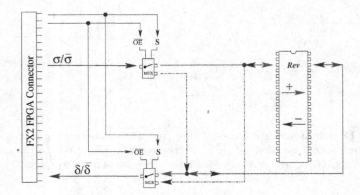

Fig. 9. Schematic showing how to use the circuit in reverse calculation. Inputs and outputs are swapped.

connected to the reversible chip's inputs and the multiplexer's first output to the reversible chip's outputs. In this configuration, the unused multiplexer outputs act as high-impedance nodes such that no short circuit occurs between the inputs and outputs of the reversible chip.

3.4   Clocking the Signals

In classical switching technology an external clock is often used. This clock signal is in the reversible DLPT technology somewhat "embedded" in the triangular shape of the input signals. The full computation performed in the reversible chip is "synchronous", but the signals propagate in an asynchronous manner from one gate to the next. In other words, the triangle waves propagate through the different gates and should arrive at the same time at the next stage of computation, without the intervention of an external clock. In practice this can not be completely guaranteed.

The clocking interfacing from the classical CMOS computing stage to the reversible computing stage, may be done by generating the dual-line triangular adiabatic signal from the classical clock, by, first, using an integrator circuit to generate one triangular pulse V_{in}, followed by a full-wave rectifier to generate the adiabatic logic "1" pulses. A simple solution to transform triangular pulses into dual-line adiabatic ones is presented in Fig. 10 [8]. These pulses are then redirected afterwards, following the method described in Section 3.1.

To synchronize the adiabatic signals coming out of the reversible stage to the classical stage is more complicated. As a solution, the amplitude of one chosen output is detected using a threshold detector and stored until the data is used. This can be done externally using flip-flops in the classical stage, after converting the adiabatic signal into classical square-wave signal, as explained in Section 3.2.

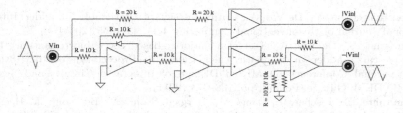

Fig. 10. Schematic of the simple circuit experimentaly used to generate the dual-line adiabatic triangular pulses from one simple triangular input

4   Conclusion

We proposed in this paper, several possible answers to the most important questions regarding the interfacing of *reversible adiabatic dual-line pass-transistor CMOS* chips with *classical restoring* circuits:

- the conversion of the pulse shape,
- the transmission of the computed information back to the FPGA,
- the reversibility of the computation,
- and the synchronization of the signals at the output interface.

For each one of these questions, at least one simple solution has been detailed and experimented, proving that embedding reversible adiabatic chips into conventional restoring circuits may be a viable yet simple solution for both, energy saving and reversibility of computation.

Acknowledgement. The authors thank the Danish Council for Strategic Research for support of this work in the framework of the MICROPOWER research project and the TECHNICAL UNIVERSITY OF ŁÓDŹ for collaboration through *Erasmus Exchanges*.

References

1. Landauer, R.: Irreversibility and heat generation in the computing process. IBM Journal of Research and Development 5(3), 183–191 (1961)
2. Von Neumann, J.: Theory of self-reproducing automata, p. 66ss. University of Illinois Press, Urbana (1966)
3. Bennett, C.H.: Logical reversibility of computation. IBM Journal of Research and Development 17(6), 525–532 (1973)
4. Fredkin, E., Toffoli, T.: Conservative logic. International Journal of Theoretical Physics 21(3-4), 219–253 (1982)
5. Feynman, R.P.: Quantum mechanical computer. Optics News 11, 11–20 (1985)
6. Desoete, B., De Vos, A., Sibiński, M., Widerski, T.: Feynman's reversible logic gates, implemented in silicon. In: Proceedings of the 6th International Conference on MIXed DESign of Integrated Circuits and Systems (MIXDES), Kraków, pp. 497–502 (June 1999)

7. Van Rentergem, Y., De Vos, A.: Optimal design of a reversible full adder. International Journal of Unconventional Computing 4(1), 339–355 (2005)
8. Burignat, S., De Vos, A.: Test of a majority-based reversible (quantum) 4 bits ripple-carry adder in adiabatic calculation. In: Proceedings of the 18th International Conference on MIXed DESign of Integrated Circuits and Systems (MIXDES), Gliwice, Poland, pp. 368–373 (2011)
9. Amirante, E., Fischer, J., Lang, M., Bargagli-Stoffi, A., Berthold, J., Heer, C., Schmitt-Landsiedel, D.: An ultra low-power adiabatic adder embedded in a standard 0.13 μm CMOS environment. In: Proceedings of the 29th European Solid-State Circuits Conference (ESSCIRC 2003), pp. 599–602 (2003)
10. De Vos, A., Burignat, S., Thomsen, M.K.: Reversible implementation of a discrete integer linear transformation. Journal of Multiple-Valued Logic and Soft Computing 18(5), 25–35 (2011)
11. Cuccaro, S., Draper, T., Moulton, D., Kutin, S.: A new quantum ripple-carry addition circuit. In: Proceedings of the 8th Workshop on Quantum Information Processing, Cambridge (June 2005); arXiv:quant-ph/0410184v, 19 pages (2004)
12. Thomsen, M.K., Glück, R., Axelsen, H.B.: Reversible Arithmetic Logic Unit for quantum arithmetic. Journal of Physics A: Mathematical and Theoretical 43, 382002ss (2010)
13. Xilinx: Spartan-3E FPGA Starter Kit Board User Guide, UG230 (v1.1), 166 pages, June 20 (2008)
14. Younis, S.G., Knight, J.T.F.: Asymptotically zero energy computing split-level charge recovery logic. In: Proceedings of the International Workshop in Low Power Design, pp.177–182 (1994)
15. Vieri, C.J.: Reversible computer engineering and architecture. PhD. Thesis, MIT 165 pages (1999)

Author Index